Your Vintage Wedding

Unique Ideas and
Inspiration for
Today's Bride

FEATURING PHOTOGRAPHS BY
Laurie Gordon

Your Vintage Wedding

Nancy Eaton

HarperResource

An Imprint of HarperCollins*Publishers*

HarperCollins books may be purchased for educational, business,
or sales promotional use. For information please write:
Special Markets Department, HarperCollins Publishers Inc.,
10 East 53rd Street, New York, NY 10022.

FIRST EDITION

Conceived and developed by Markel Waggoner Books

Printed on acid-free paper

Library of Congress Cataloging-in-Publication Data has been applied for.

ISBN 0-688-17753-0

01 02 03 04 05 Imago 10 9 8 7 6 5 4 3 2 1

For Mom, who was a beautiful 1940s bride,

and for Dad—I wish you could have seen this.

Contents

Acknowledgments

our Vintage Wedding would not have been possible without the efforts of Toni Sciarra and Eula Biss of HarperCollins Publishers and Jacqueline Deval of Hearst Books. I'd also like to thank Bob Markel and Susan Waggoner for helping to make this book a reality.

Many people contributed invaluable information, materials, and photographs for this book. Thanks to Laurie Gordon for her amazing talent, generosity, and dedication to all things vintage. Thanks also to Mary Litzinger, Donna Barr, Deborah Burke, Lauren Lavonne Pritchett, Phyllis Magidson, Dawn Boehmer, Theresa LaQuey, Lisa Grable, Gary Chapman, Lisa Scovel, Charliene Felts, Betty Skel, Karen Armstrong, Christopher Bunn, Alice Leamy, Drew McEachern, Carolyn Kirsch, and Peter Lalli. And, of course, thanks to all the wonderful brides and grooms who shared their stories and appear in these pages. I'd also like to thank those who took the time to contribute photos and stories that unfortunately could not be included.

Generous thanks to photographers Laurie Gordon, Steve Streble, Ralph Granich, and Cary Shapiro, and to the anonymous and long-departed wedding photographers who shot the original vintage portraits used in this book.

*Your
Vintage
Wedding*

Something Old, Something Older

hen Tonya Castleman got engaged, she decided to do something different for her wedding, something that reflected her personal sense of style. "I think we're influenced from childhood to believe that a wedding has to be a certain way," said Castleman. "I definitely didn't want to do the typical thing, with the poofy-sleeved dress and the tuxedo with the ruffled shirt. That just wasn't me. One day I was flipping through my grandmother's wedding album. She looked so elegant and gorgeous, I decided right then and there that I just had to have a 1930s wedding."

(Photo: Laurie Gordon)

Castleman is one of a growing number of contemporary brides who have fallen in love with vintage twentieth-century romance and style. Besides that extra soupçon of romance it brings to an already romantic day, a vintage wedding is a meaningful and entertaining experience for the entire wedding party and unexpected fun for your wedding guests—all of whom will reflect on a most memorable event for many years to come.

A "HOW TO" GUIDE FOR VINTAGE WEDDINGS

espite an enormous interest in vintage culture among contemporary brides- and grooms-to-be, it's not easy to learn how to plan and execute a wedding with classic twentieth-century elements. "I found out plenty about having a Victorian event," Castleman says, "but there was very little I could find about 1930s weddings. Researching the period details was definitely the hardest part."

We plan to change all that. *Your Vintage Wedding* is a guide to the twentieth-century periods that are proving to be enduring classics with contemporary brides. These periods include the Art Nouveau elegance of the 1910s; the Art Deco glamour of the 1920s and 1930s; the nightclub and café society and tropical trends of the 1930s and 1940s; and the abstract-modern culture of the 1950s, including Audrey Hepburn chic and maybe a touch of Vegas tossed in for good measure.

We'll give you an overview of what weddings were like in these past decades and examine specific elements of a wedding that can be enhanced with vintage touches. We'll also share ideas we learned from vintage event consultants, florists, caterers, photographers, printers, dressmakers, and antique clothing dealers—and from couples who are planning vintage weddings or have had them in the past few years.

For some couples a vintage wedding means adding a touch or two here and there, but for others it means planning a historically accurate event, right down to the tiniest details. It's really up to you, limited only by your personal preferences, your time frame, and the size of your pocketbook.

ANYTHING GOES

ong before Martha Stewart was decorating her diapers, the reigning doyennes of gracious living and etiquette were Emily Post and Amy Vanderbilt, and their nuptial dos and don'ts dictated wedding behavior for decades. But today brides have far more creative latitude. It's perfectly appropriate to have nontraditional wedding invitations, wear any color or style of wedding dress, have a ceremony in Grand Central Station, or deck out your groomsmen in zoot suits. What Cole Porter astutely declared in the 1920s applies even more so today: "Anything goes."

Before you get started, ask yourself a few questions: Do you have an idea which era appeals to you most? How historically accurate do you want to be? Would you like a formal or an informal wedding? What kind of budget do you have to work with? And most important: How much time do you have until the wedding?

Naturally, if you have a big budget and a lot of time, you can incorporate many more details into the day. But even if your finances are tight and time is relatively short, don't be too concerned, because there's still a lot that you can do. If you have no idea where to start, don't worry about that, either, as this book was designed to help stimulate your creative juices.

Whatever your reasons for wanting a vintage wedding, we know from experience that you'll realize benefits far beyond what you expect. So let us help make your special day even more so by inviting the past to be an honored guest at your wedding.

(Photo: Laurie Gordon)

The Way They Wed: 1910s–1950s

The etiquette of the formal wedding is not just a hodgepodge of arbitrary rules, but a beautifully integrated procedure handed down to you by generations of happy brides.

—Barbara T. Morrow, wedding counselor, 1950

t's surprising how many long-standing wedding traditions started out as ancient pagan rituals, conceived as a way to bring luck or to protect a couple from evil spirits. Some of these traditions live on today, seamlessly blended into what Morrow called the "integrated procedure" of a wedding.

But despite a lasting set of well-worn traditions, weddings look different from decade to decade because of the prevailing trends in fashion, popular culture, political events, and accepted social behavior. Trends influence new wedding traditions and even cause some of the old standbys to fall out of favor.

Let's take a look at the trends and influences that shaped the 1910s through the 1950s and see how these were reflected in the weddings of each period. Perhaps you'll discover a few forgotten traditions to revive for your special day.

THE 1910S

his was a decade of emancipation for women—they shortened their skirts, loosened their corsets, and got the vote. However, the biggest event that affected everyone was the Great War, which devastated Europe for seven years, starting in 1912.

But the 1910s was also a beautiful decade. Art Nouveau dominated the decorative arts, with an emphasis on graceful forms and stylistic elements derived from nature. This was also the decade in which certain turn-of-the-century technological advances became commonplace conveniences, including automobiles, telephones, phonographs, and electricity.

The growing popularity of the automobile meant that people could travel greater distances for leisure and entertainment. Wealthy couples ventured out of town by car or train to hold their weddings at country clubs or estates. Some newlyweds went on motoring honeymoons, touring the countryside in their new automobiles; and the wealthiest trekked back and forth to Europe on luxury ocean liners.

Whether at home or out of town, many fashionable weddings took place outdoors in formal gardens. Even if a wedding was held indoors, it was decorated with garden scenery, including lots of wicker furniture, flowers, hanging ferns, and potted palms.

At the beginning of the 1910s, Paris still remained the world's fashion center. But after the Great War broke out in Europe in 1912, brides on this side of the Atlantic had to make do without their Parisian gowns. They turned to domestic designers, seamstresses, and home sewing as an alternative. The full economic impact of the Great War didn't hit America until late in the decade, but by 1917 and 1918 fabric shortages were finally felt in the United States, when seamstresses were limited to using just 4.5 yards of cloth per dress.

In the 1910s, dancer Irene Castle and her husband and partner, Vernon, had everyone dancing the new fox trot, turkey trot, Castle gavotte, and tango. The first commercial blues songs were recorded in the 1910s, and in 1915 Hawaiian music was brought to America for the Panama Pacific Exposition in San Francisco.

The Victorian era technically ended in 1901, but American women didn't rid themselves of its corseted "S-shaped" silhouette until about seven years later. Women then turned to wearing straight, slender dresses with high, wide "Empire" waistlines, a design inspired by the clothing of French couturier Paul Poirot. Dresses with Grecian influence and

Typical informal 1910s wedding clothing.

A late 1910s bride displays her shower bouquet.

tunic overskirts were popular in silk chiffon, silk charmeuse, gauzes, and heavy silk satins—and always worn with ropes and ropes of pearls. Some evening gowns had long, trailing panels that formed a train.

In the early 1910s, hemlines rose above the ankles for the first time, although wedding gowns and evening dresses were worn longer.

The most popular style of wedding veil had floor-length tulle falling from a cluster of flowers atop the bride's head. Orange blossoms were a perennial favorite. The upswept Gibson girl hairdo continued to be popular until Irene Castle bobbed her hair in mid-decade, causing a fad for short hairstyles that lasted until the end of the 1920s.

The new rage for brides was the "shower bouquet," with flowers loosely and casually arranged and streamers of ribbons and vines trailing almost to the floor. The most popular

Early 1910s garden dresses and flower baskets, a perfect look for bridesmaids.

wedding flowers were white roses, white lilies of the valley, white orchids, gardenias, and orange blossoms.

Bridesmaids typically wore evening or garden-party dresses, depending on the formality of the wedding. Some brides had their attendants all dress alike, starting a popular new trend. On their heads bridesmaids wore wreaths of flowers or the large hats popular during this time.

The groom's wedding outfit varied depending on the formality of the wedding and the time of day. Up until World War I, some grooms at formal weddings still wore frock coats, a longtime favorite of nineteenth-century men. Frock coats were long jackets that extended to midcalf, typically worn with gray pants, a top hat, and tan or white shoes and spats.

The standard formal daytime wedding attire was the morning coat with striped trousers, a starched white shirt and collar, and a black top hat with a curve on one or both sides. For formal evening weddings, men wore tail-

POPULAR MUSICIANS OF THE 1910S
Irving Berlin
Eubie Blake
W. C. Handy
Al Jolson
Jelly Roll Morton
Bessie Smith
Ethel Waters

POPULAR SONGS OF THE 1910S
"Ah! Sweet Mystery of Life"
"Be My Little Baby Bumblebee"
"If You Were the Only Girl in the World"
"Jelly Roll Blues"
"Let Me Call You Sweetheart"
"Let the Rest of the World Go By"
"A Pretty Girl Is Like a Melody"
"A Ring on the Finger Is Worth Two on the Phone"
"Rock-a-Bye Your Baby with a Dixie Melody"
"St. Louis Blues"
"To Have, to Hold, to Love"
"Twelfth Street Rag"

A 1910s groom sports a formal frock coat, top hat, and gloves.

coats with white waistcoats (vests), ties, gloves, and a black top hat. Shirts had raised and pointed collars.

Grooms at more informal weddings wore a dark blue three-button suit with a white or dark waistcoat to match the jacket. This was worn with a white shirt with a starched, rounded collar and a white tie and gloves. Hats were optional.

THE 1920S

he Eighteenth Amendment passed in 1920, forbidding the sale and consumption of alcohol in the United States and pooping parties everywhere until this unpopular law was repealed in 1933. The public flouted Prohibition, so it's likely that more than one 1920s wedding punch was spiked with a little bathtub gin or Veuve Clicquot. Couples danced the Charleston and the black bottom until the joint was raided and everybody had to go home.

Skirt lengths reached an all-time high in 1925 when they hit the knee. Women wore undergarments to flatten their breasts or wore very little underneath their clothing at all. Jazz was all the rage, Hollywood's star was rising, and the world belonged to the young and carefree.

Fashion and decor were strongly influenced by Chinese and Egyptian motifs and rich, jewel-tone colors, and in 1925 the Exposition des Arts Décoratifs in Paris catapulted French-style Art Deco and modernism into the world.

Miami and Honolulu were the hot new honeymoon destinations for Americans, but the perennial favorite was still Niagara Falls, where the first person to go over the waterfall in a barrel (a woman, incidentally) did so in the early 1920s.

Short wedding dresses were all the rage for both formal and informal weddings, although brides wore wedding gowns slightly longer than day dresses. Some gowns had unusual hemlines, with scalloped edges or handkerchief points. Most had dropped waists, with belt lines low at the hip. Some were softly draped, gathered up and pinned on one side, either with real flowers or artificial ones made of wax or silk. Many gowns had no sleeves, with rounded or V-shaped necks in the front and back, or lace bodice inserts with long lace sleeves. Popular fabrics included silk satins, silk crepes, silk velvets, and lace. Brides in the 1920s typically did not wear gloves.

The most popular shoes were pumps, with or without a T-strap, made of silk or soft kid, with a slightly rounded toe and a medium-curved heel. Wedding hose was made of silk and colored white, ivory, or soft beige, and a new fad was to wear stockings with jeweled designs on the ankle or calf.

The quintessential mid-1920s bride.

Women idealized the exotic and glamorous Hollywood silent stars who influenced a trend toward dramatic and theatrical wedding clothing. Shown: Gloria Swanson in Her Love Story *(1924).*
(Photo: Corbis)

As skirts got shorter, wedding bouquets got larger, with trailing streamers of ribbon tied with lovers' knots and greenery. Some brides even heightened the theatrics by trimming their bouquets Hollywood style, with fur, egret or marabou feathers, or ostrich plumes.

Wedding portraits from the 1920s show brides wearing a variety of head-pieces. The most popular styles included bandeaux, crownlike diadem tiaras of lace or pearls, wreaths of orange blossoms, or cloche caps made of lace.

Typical bridal headgear of the 1920s.

Sew-it-yourself wedding attire
from Simplicity, 1927.

*Bride and groom in 1920s
formal daytime attire.*

Veils were worn extremely long and were usually made of simple tulle.

Hollywood inspired the most popular hairstyles, including the short, geo-metric shingle bob worn by popular silent film stars Colleen Moore and Louise Brooks and the wispy windblown bob worn by Clara Bow, the "It" girl. Women powdered their faces pale and wore red lipstick imitating the pouty, kewpie-doll "bee-stung" lips of movie stars such as Mae Murray.

Bridesmaids wore evening-style dresses of the period, and most of them

Friends of the bride and groom enjoyed playing pranks on the couple, including decorating the getaway car and tying shoes and tin cans to the bumper.

wore matching outfits. Most bridesmaids' dresses were sleeveless, calf length, with dropped waists and asymmetrical hemlines. Bridesmaids usually did not wear gloves.

Their headpieces consisted of floral wreaths or hats with deep crowns and large brims. After 1923, tight-fitting cloche hats were all the rage. Cloches came about as the result of the open automobile: hats needed to fit snugly in order not to blow away.

Most bridesmaids carried bouquets similar to the bride's, but slightly smaller and a different color. Baskets of flowers were also popular, especially for garden or informal weddings.

Grooms generally wore the same clothes as in the 1910s, with the exception of the frock coat, which by then had gone out of style. The cutaway coat

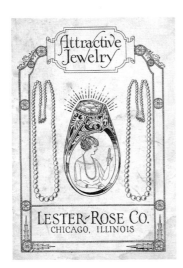

Lester-Rose Jewelry Catalog, 1920s.

POPULAR MUSICIANS OF THE 1920S

Louis Armstrong
Bix Beiderbecke
Eubie Blake
Cab Calloway
Eddie Cantor
Duke Ellington
Fletcher Henderson
Alberta Hunter
Al Jolson
Jimmie Lunceford
Jelly Roll Morton
Original Dixieland Jazz Band
Sophie Tucker
Rudy Vallee
Fats Waller
Ethel Waters
Paul Whiteman

POPULAR SONGS OF THE 1920S

"Ain't Misbehavin' "
"Ain't We Got Fun"
"Always"
"The Best Things in Life Are Free"
"The Birth of the Blues"
"Fascinating Rhythm"
"Happy Days Are Here Again"
"Honeysuckle Rose"
"I Can't Give You Anything but Love"
"I'm Just Wild About Harry"
"I'm Sitting on Top of the World"
"Ma! He's Making Eyes at Me!"
"Makin' Whoopee"
"The Man I Love"
"Me and My Shadow"
"(Oh) Lady Be Good"
"Say It with Music"
"Singin' in the Rain"
"Somebody Loves Me"
"Someone to Watch Over Me"
"Stardust"
" 'S Wonderful"
"With a Song in My Heart"
"Yes Sir, That's My Baby"
"You're the Cream in My Coffee"
"You've Gotta See Mamma Ev'ry Night, Or You Can't See Mamma at All"

was the correct choice for formal daytime weddings. The modern 1920s groom also may have sported a wristwatch, a brand-new fashion trend started by film legend Rudolph Valentino in 1921.

THE 1930S

he Great Depression was financially devastating, and most Americans reacted by tightening their belts and getting by the best they could.

Young people postponed their nuptials, causing the marriage rate to drop 13 percent between 1930 and 1932. By the end of the decade the average age at first marriage was more than twenty-six years, an increase of two years for both men and women.

As a result of the Depression, most working-class weddings were austere affairs, held at home or at a place of worship, followed by modest family celebrations. Only the most privileged couples could afford receptions at country clubs, hotel ballrooms, or country estates.

In July 1938 *LOOK* magazine compared the weddings of two brides-to-be: one wealthy and one average. According to *LOOK*, the wealthy woman spent up to $300 for a custom-designed dress and headpiece (about $6,000 today), while the average woman spent $15 to $30 for a dress (about $300 to $600 today). The wealthy woman was shown working with a caterer to plan refreshments for a wedding reception with hundreds of guests, while the average woman was shown buying fruit for a simple reception punch.

Champagne flowed freely at weddings as well as in nightclubs after Prohibition ended in 1933. Couples danced the Lindy hop to big band and swing music, spawned by the Harlem Renaissance of the late 1920s. For escapist entertainment, people flocked to the new talking pictures, where everyone was drop-dead gorgeous and nobody seemed to suffer from an empty wallet. They sought refuge in the glamour of Garbo and Harlow, the wit of Nick and Nora Charles from the *Thin Man* series, the dapper elegance of Fred and Ginger, the musicals of Busby Berkeley, and the wackiness of the Marx Brothers, among many others. At home the radio was the primary source of entertainment, featuring nonstop music, variety shows, and serials.

Weddings became such a romantic and popular subject with young women by the end of the 1930s that the first magazines were published exclusively for brides-to-be. *The Bride's* magazine showcased the latest styles for the bride's gown and trousseau, dictating the proper wedding etiquette, providing honeymoon ideas, and helping young women equip home and hearth in anticipation of happily married life to come.

In the early 1930s, brides wore slim and form-fitting gowns cut on the bias, with gored skirts made of silk or lace. Some wedding gowns featured fuller skirts, including layers of lace or tulle. Silk satins and silk velvets were popular fabrics, with rayon crepe-backed satin making a strong showing by the end of the decade. Although the slim 1930s bridal silhouette was inspired by the seductive evening gowns of the period, most wedding gowns had conservative necklines and didn't expose the back or bosom.

Wedding dresses were worn floor length, with formal gowns having long trains, sometimes elaborately decorated. Long gloves made an elegant comeback after an absence of several decades, worn with short-sleeved or sleeveless wedding dresses.

The first matching wedding and engagement ring sets appeared in 1930 as part of a marketing campaign by the diamond industry.

The "sweetheart" neckline first appeared in the late 1930s and was a popular element of women's clothing until the 1950s. Attractive and flattering to most figure types, the neckline was sometimes set off by fancy matching dress clips worn on either side.

An early 1930s bride in lace and tulle, with long gloves, Juliet cap, and shower bouquet.

Divorcée Wallis Simpson wed the dashing Duke of Windsor (Prince Edward VII) in June 1937, after he abdicated the throne to marry her. The elegant long-sleeved Mainbocher gown she wore was widely copied, hitting London shops within days after the couple took their vows. (Photo: Corbis)

The most popular wedding headpiece of the early 1930s was the Juliet cap—a small skullcap, usually made of lace, worn on the back of the head and anchored to the veil at each side by a spray of orange blossoms, lilies of the valley, or other small flowers. Another popular headpiece was coronet shaped, resembling the rays of the sun. Veils were simple, single or double layered, and worn very long.

Women wore their hair slightly longer than they did in the 1920s, loosely waved and parted on the side. For dressy occasions in the late 1930s, women wore upswept hairdos with curls piled high on top of their heads. They con-

A mid-1930s formal wedding party.

tinued to wear bright red lipstick and plucked their eyebrows severely, penciling in high, thin arches. On their fingertips women followed a fad for brightly painted nails with contrasting white cuticle "moons" and nail tips.

Bridal fashion continued to be inspired by Hollywood. The 1938 Bette Davis film *Jezebel* and 1939's *Gone With the Wind* inspired a brief flirtation with antebellum styles, and gowns sported such old-fashioned elements as bows, ruffles, hoop skirts, and multiple petticoats. Fashion designers also revived the late Victorian period, adding details such as bustles and leg-o'-mutton sleeves.

Joan Crawford started a craze for enormous puffed sleeves, which became a favorite detail of wedding gowns and bridesmaid's dresses throughout the 1930s. Bridesmaids wore long dresses of rayon or silk, in chiffons, satins, taffetas, moirés, or velvets. Evening dresses, including the floral silk chiffon bias-cut dresses of the early 1930s, with their tiny Art Deco rhinestone belt buckles, were also classic and elegant selections for any wedding party.

Shoes worn by brides and bridesmaids were similar to those from the 1920s, made of silk or kid with narrow ankle straps or T-straps, but with straighter and higher heels and slightly rounder toes. Some evening shoes were adorned with decorative jeweled buckles. High-heeled, open-toed sandals in metallic shades were very glamorous for evening wear, and some brides chose to wear these colors instead of the traditional white or ivory.

Classic men's wedding attire still included the cutaway coat and the tailcoat. But even though the etiquette mistresses didn't approve, some grooms began adopting a semiformal look, wearing tuxedos with black or white ties and waistcoats. For casual weddings, men wore double-breasted dark blue

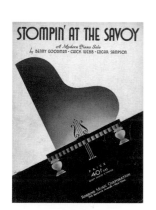

POPULAR MUSICIANS OF THE 1930S

Louis Armstrong
Fred Astaire
Count Basie
Cab Calloway
Maurice Chevalier
Bing Crosby
Jimmy Dorsey
Tommy Dorsey
Duke Ellington
Ella Fitzgerald
Benny Goodman
Lionel Hampton
Billie Holiday
Harry James
Gene Krupa
Glenn Miller
Jack Teagarden
Chick Webb

POPULAR SONGS OF THE 1930S

"All the Things You Are"
"Begin the Beguine"
"Body and Soul"
"Cheek to Cheek"
"Dream a Little Dream of Me"
"Ebb Tide"
"Embraceable You"
"Falling in Love with Love"
"A Foggy Day"
"Harbor Lights"
"How Deep Is the Ocean?"
"I Cover the Waterfront"
"I Didn't Know What Time It Was"
"I Get a Kick out of You"
"I Got Rhythm"
"I'm in the Mood for Love"
"In the Chapel in the Moonlight"
"In the Still of the Night"
"I Only Have Eyes for You"
"It Don't Mean a Thing If It Ain't Got That Swing"
"I Told Every Little Star"

*Some 1930s grooms broke
with tradition by wearing
tuxedos.*

"It's Only a Paper Moon"
"I've Got My Love to Keep Me
    Warm"
"I've Got You Under My Skin"
"Let's Face the Music and Dance"
"Let's Fall in Love"
"Let Yourself Go"
"Love Walked In"
"Mood Indigo"
"Moonglow"
"My Funny Valentine"
"Night and Day"
"The Night Is Young and You're So
    Beautiful"

"Over the Rainbow"
"Pennies from Heaven"
"Puttin' on the Ritz"
"Shall We Dance?"
"Sing, Sing, Sing"
"Smoke Gets in Your Eyes"
"Stairway to the Stars"
"St. James Infirmary"
"Stompin' at the Savoy"
"Sunrise Serenade"
"Temptation"
"Thanks for the Memory"
"These Foolish Things Remind Me
    of You"

"Three Little Words"
"The Very Thought of You"
"The Way You Look Tonight"
"What a Diff'rence a Day Made"
"What Is This Thing Called Love?"
"You and the Night and the Music"
"You Brought a New Kind of Love to
    Me"
"You Must Have Been a Beautiful
    Baby"
"You're an Old Smoothie"
"You're the Top"
"Zing Went the Strings of My Heart"

suits with wide, cuffed trousers. And for outdoor summer weddings, they wore single-breasted gabardine Palm Beach suits with Panama hats.

THE 1940S

etween 1940 and 1942, one thousand World War II servicemen and their fiancées got married every day, often while the groom was on furlough. According to *Vogue,* a 1942 wartime wedding was ". . . a quick wedding, nine times out of ten. It means setting the date at the drop of a telegram; making arrangements practically overnight; shopping for a wedding dress while the champagne cools for the reception."

The U.S. War Production Board placed restrictions on most clothing, but surprisingly, wedding gowns were exempt. Brides could wear gowns of any length and material, but many opted to make a patriotic sacrifice by wearing short cocktail dresses or suits instead. *The Bride's* magazine suggested a few appropriate fabric choices in autumn 1946: "Ever since the first war bride wore a dress from a parachute, you've learned that you may use nylon, lingerie satin, thin crepes, cottons, upholstery brocades as substitutes for the traditional tissues."

Although natural fabrics were legal to wear in America, they were in short supply both during and after the war. Some countries outside the United States had strict rationing laws that continued even into the 1950s. Royalty wasn't even spared the inconvenience, as Great Britain's Princess Elizabeth was required to cash in clothing ration coupons to obtain enough yardage for her silk wedding dress and bridesmaids' gowns when she married Prince Philip in 1947.

The war in the South Pacific inspired a fad for tropical culture in the United States that extended to home decorating, entertainment, and clothing. Floral Hawaiian-print sportswear for men and women was very popular, and the flattering draped sarongs popularized by Dorothy Lamour were incorporated into everything from swimsuits to day and evening wear. After the war ended, honeymooning couples resumed their peacetime pilgrimages to Hawaii on the familiar ocean liners as well as by air on the China Clipper.

A 1945 bride in an informal cotton eyelet gown, her sailor groom in uniform.

*After the war ended, ads for new
"pink champagne" wedding dresses
appeared in brides' magazines.
Marketed to older brides or for
second weddings, these gowns were
slow to catch on and didn't do so
until the early 1950s.*

Before, during, and after the war, young adults flocked to nightclubs, where everybody was dancing the conga and the mambo, popularized by bandleaders Xavier Cugat and Desi Arnaz. The Lindy hop was still the dance of choice for most young people, who swung to big band music fronted by such vocalists as Frank Sinatra and Ella Fitzgerald. And Harlem musicians, including Louis Jordan and Wynonie Harris, performed their breed of up-tempo music known as jump blues, a precursor of rock 'n' roll.

Women who chose long gowns usually wore rayon crepe-backed satin or taffeta, as silk was needed to make parachutes. Cotton eyelet gowns were popular for informal summer weddings. Dresses had details such as peplums, straight skirts, and slightly nipped-in princess waists and were usually fitted at the neckline, wrist, waist, and midriff. The sweetheart neckline remained a favorite throughout the decade.

Brides wearing formal wedding gowns continued to prefer the arched coronet headpiece of fabric or lace. Veils consisted of several layers of tulle in varying lengths, with a bit of gathering at the crown for height and volume. For informal weddings when brides wore trainless gowns, the veils were usually shorter, sometimes falling from a band of flowers in the bride's hair.

Brides who married in suits or dresses usually wore a hat with a short veil or flowers in their hair. For daytime, women parted their shoulder-length hair on the side and curled the ends and the bangs. For dressy occasions, they swept it up on top of their head and arranged it in rolls or curls or wore it long and curled under, gathered in a snood.

The shower, or cascading, bouquet was still the favorite style, but it was smaller than in the 1920s or 1930s. The streamers and lovers' knots started

A 1940s bride in a rayon taffeta suit, her hat adorned with orange blossoms.
(Photo: George Fries)

27

A trio of 1940s bridesmaids in patterned rayon taffeta.

(Photo: Alice Leamy)

disappearing, as they were now considered old-fashioned. Instead of bouquets, some brides carried armloads of flowers tied with ribbons.

Shoes looked chunkier than in the 1930s and had rounded toes that were open or closed, with slingbacks or regular backs. Platform shoes of varying heights were also popular, with high-heeled strappy platform sandals a big hit for day or evening.

For traditional weddings, bridesmaids wore long dresses, and it was fashionable for them to be made in a style that mimicked the bride's dress. For semiformal and informal weddings, brides often chose practical dresses for their bridesmaids that the women could wear again for other occasions. For informal weddings, bridesmaids wore dresses or suits if the bride did the same.

An early 1940s formal military wedding.

Groom and best man in semiformal white dinner jackets, late 1940s.

Men in the armed services often wore their uniforms at their weddings and chose groomsmen who were also in the military services. Grooms in uniform wore their sidearms, but not their caps. None of the military members of a wedding wore boutonnieres. After the ceremony, groomsmen would draw their sabers and form an arch, under which the couple passed in the recessional.

THREE TYPICAL WEDDINGS, 1940S STYLE

In 1942 author Marjorie Binford Woods offered budgets for several sample weddings in her book *Your Wedding: How to Plan and Enjoy It*. The following examples are interesting not only to learn what wedding goods and services cost at the time, but to find out the elements that went into 1940s weddings of varying degrees of formality. (*Note:* multiply by 10 to 15 to approximate today's equivalent costs.)

Semiformal Home Wedding, with a Reception Outside at Home for 50 Guests

Invitations by telephone: No cost	
Trainless wedding gown and veil:	$30
Shoes, hose, and lingerie:	$10
Trousseau:	$75
Music: No cost (friends played the piano)	
Bride's cake in the shape of a wedding ring, with daisies in the center:	$20
Ice cream in wedding ring molds, with nosegays of daisies at each place setting:	$12
Daisy-shaped mints:	$2
Flower decorations: No cost (from the garden)	
Ten white candles:	$1
Bridesmaids' luncheon (4 bridesmaids):	$10
Attendants and musicians' gifts (daisy-shaped compacts in enamel):	$10
One pair *point d'esprit* curtains for tablecloth:	$3
Photographs: No cost (taken by friends)	
Florist's bill for greenery at altar, garlands for bridesmaids:	$12
Incidentals, including maid to serve refreshments, thank-you notepaper, white cocktail napkins, and so on:	$15
Total	*$200*

A Formal Wedding, Held at Church, Followed by a Reception at Home for 100 People

Bridal ensemble: $100	
(gown $50; veil $25; shoes, hose, and slip $25)	
Trousseau:	$125
Florist: (for tulips, in season)	$125
Invitations:	$75
(white vellum paper engraved in shaded roman)	
Bridesmaids' Luncheon:	$25
(given by the bride's mother at home four days before the wedding)	
Bridesmaids' gifts:	$30
(jeweled clips for 3 attendants)	
Reception refreshments and catering:	$125
(domestic champagne punch and tea sandwiches for 100 guests)	
Music (church and reception):	$40
(organist fee at church $20, harpist for reception $20)	
Bride's cake:	$50
(three tiers with decoration of wedding bells on top)	
Photos and incidentals:	$55
Total	*$750*

A Formal Cathedral Wedding for 1,500 Guests, with a Reception for 200 at a Large Hotel

Invitations and announcements:	$200
Floral decorations (including canopy) for bridal dinner, church, hotel:	$196
Rehearsal dinner at club (for 48 guests at $3 per plate):	$144
Bridesmaids' gifts and accessories, plus headdresses (for 5):	$100
Transportation for the wedding party:	$50
Music at church and reception:	$100
Bride's cake and boxed wedding cake souvenirs:	$90
Wedding gown and veil:	$200
Lingerie:	$120
Personal trousseau:	$500
Reception (200 guests at $2.25 per person):	$450
Photography and incidentals:	$150
Total	*$2,300*

In the 1940s, civilian middle-class men examined their choices for wedding attire and found something lacking. For many, the traditional tailcoats and cutaway coats were impractical and far too formal. On the other hand, a business suit often wasn't formal enough, especially if the bride was wearing a long gown and the wedding was after six. As a result, many grooms

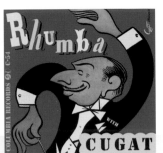

Courtesy of Sony Records

POPULAR MUSICIANS OF THE 1940S

Andrews Sisters
Louis Armstrong
Desi Arnaz
Count Basie
Tex Beneke
Nat "King" Cole
Bing Crosby
Xavier Cugat
Vic Damone
Jimmy Dorsey
Tommy Dorsey
Billy Eckstine
Duke Ellington
Ella Fitzgerald
Benny Goodman
Dick Haymes
Woody Herman
The Ink Spots
Louis Jordan
Stan Kenton
Frankie Laine
Jimmie Lunceford
Glenn Miller
Vaughn Monroe
Helen O'Connell
Artie Shaw
Dinah Shore
Frank Sinatra
Jack Teagarden
Mel Tormé
Dinah Washington

POPULAR SONGS OF THE 1940S

"A String of Pearls"
"Baby, It's Cold Outside"
"Besame Mucho"
"But Beautiful"
"By the Light of the Silvery Moon"
"Come Rain or Come Shine"
"Don't Sit Under the Apple Tree"
"Everything I Have Is Yours"
"A Fellow Needs a Girl"
"How High the Moon"
"I Couldn't Sleep a Wink Last Night"
"I Got the Sun in the Morning"
"I Hear a Rhapsody"
"It Might as Well Be Spring"
"It's a Big, Wide, Wonderful World"
"(I Love You) For Sentimental Reasons"
"The Last Time I Saw Paris"
"Moonlight Becomes You"
"The More I See You"
"My Happiness"
"The Nearness of You"
"Paper Doll"
"Peg o' My Heart"
"Pennsylvania 6-5000"
"Serenade in Blue"
"So in Love"
"Some Enchanted Evening"
"Taking a Chance on Love"
"Tenderly"
"There! I've Said It Again"
"This Love of Mine"
"Time Waits for No One"
"We'll Meet Again"
"When You Wish Upon a Star"
"You Are My Sunshine"
"You'd Be So Nice to Come Home To"
"You Made Me Love You"
"You Stepped out of a Dream"

rejected tradition and went to the altar wearing the accepted semiformal attire of the day—tuxedos or white dinner jackets.

THE 1950S

hroughout this prosperous decade, marriage rates were high and brides kept getting younger every year. By 1959, 47 percent of all first-time brides were less than nineteen years old—a statistic that might be explained by the prevailing cultural premium placed on chastity and conservatism.

Television was brand new, and viewers got to compare themselves with such nearly perfect TV families as the Nelsons (*Ozzie and Harriet*) and the Cleavers (*Leave It to Beaver*)—as well as the wacky (and somewhat less perfect) Ricardos (*I Love Lucy*) and Kramdens (*The Honeymooners*). Inspired by television myth, middle-class brides-to-be envisioned a perfect storybook wedding, followed by a house in the suburbs, two cars in the garage, a commuting husband, a couple of kids, and a dog—all of it expertly managed by a smiling housewife who cooked and cleaned for her family wearing a sensible shirtwaist dress, a frilly apron, and a string of pearls.

Weddings were now big business. Bridal magazines gained influence, and advertisers drove the trends. Ultraformal weddings were the rage, and brides hung on to every word set down by Emily Post and Amy Vanderbilt when planning and executing the details. More and more couples of modest means had receptions that included food, cocktails, and dancing for all the guests, even though most were still simple cake-and-punch affairs. American couples of modest means hit such hot honeymoon spots as Miami Beach, Niagara Falls, or resorts in the Pocono Mountains featuring round beds and heart-shaped bathtubs.

The 1950s ushered in hi-fi and stereophonic sound, 33 and 45 rpm records, the death of big band music, and the birth of rock 'n' roll. Teenagers embraced the new music to the chagrin of their parents, who preferred the popular easy-listening vocalists of the period.

The early 1950s saw a fad for everything French, from poodles to berets to

Early 1950s formal daytime wedding attire.

A 1950s groom sports a trendy flattop.

ballet, which influenced clothing design and women's hairstyles. Another important trend was a move toward home furnishings created by some of the leading abstract artists and designers of the day. Some of the shapes incorporated into everyday furniture, accessories, and fabrics were influenced by popular motifs used in the atomic and space race and by the abstract geometric shapes used in midcentury abstract modern art and architecture.

For the first time in the twentieth century, wedding gown manufacturers stopped basing their designs on the most popular styles of day or evening wear. As a result, some of the most beautiful formal wear of the 1950s (such as Audrey Hepburn's gown in *Sabrina*) was never translated into wedding attire. Instead, designers preferred to create Cinderella-like fantasy confections, inspired by clothing of earlier centuries, with fitted bodices, cinched-in waistlines, and voluminous skirts.

To wear these dresses properly, a bride needed to wear layers of hoop-skirted petticoats or the combination of a cinch-waist corset and a foundation garment called a bombast, which made the dress spring out from the waist. Formal gowns had long trains; informal gowns had short trains or none at all.

Most dresses advertised in bridal magazines were made of various weaves

Early 1950s semiformal daytime wedding attire. (Photo: Walter Leamy)

of rayon, although silk was still the first choice of wealthier brides. Many gowns were adorned with yards and yards of Chantilly, Venise, or French Alençon lace.

Magazine ads from the early 1950s indicated a trend for wedding gowns with high necklines, a small collar (round, pointed, or stand-up), tiny covered buttons up the front of a tight-fitting lace bodice, long lace sleeves, a fitted waist, and a bouffant skirt. Amy Vanderbilt directed a nod to this style in her 1952 wedding guide: "A wedding gown should follow a certain decorum—neckline conservative and sleeves preferably long."

Bridal magazines suggested that brides have their headpieces custom-made by copying a favorite hat in white velvet, lace, net, or satin. Veils were multitiered and gathered tightly to look "poufy" in order to complement and

Jacqueline Kennedy's silk faille gown from 1953 was one of the most elegant formal wedding gowns of the twentieth century. John F. Kennedy wore a traditional cutaway coat.

(Photo: Corbis)

Short wedding dresses were revived in the 1950s but weren't as popular as they were in the 1920s.

balance the bouffant wedding skirts. Veils were short, medium, or long, depending on the formality of the gown and what was flattering to the bride.

American women adopted the look currently popular with young French women—a short, layered boyish haircut known as the pixie or the poodle cut. Many young Hollywood stars influenced this "gamine look," including Shirley MacLaine, Leslie Caron, and Audrey Hepburn. Women with longer hair also emulated French women by wearing it pulled back in sophisticated chignons fastened with decorative combs and barrettes.

On their feet, brides from the early 1950s wore opera pumps or simple one-strap sandals, with medium to high straight heels and very round toes. One early 1950s footwear manufacturer made single-strap shoes for weddings with artificial orange blossoms worn at the ankle. Later in the decade, rounded toes were replaced by sharp, pointed tips. Heels remained high but were thin and "spiked."

By this time, the shower bouquet was considered passé. Brides preferred the small, neat, round nosegays last seen in Victorian times, armfuls of calla lilies or white roses, or a prayer book with tiny flower sprays. According to

The Bride and Home-maker in 1956, the most popular wedding flowers of the 1950s were white orchids and stephanotis. Informal wedding bouquets often included chrysanthemums, white snapdragons, or white larkspur.

Short wedding dresses were in style for the first time since the 1920s but were not as popular as the longer gowns. Inspired by ballerina costumes, the short dresses were calf length, featuring tight waists and wide skirts, with layers of tulle and crinoline

Most 1950s bridesmaids wore short, "ballerina-length" dresses.

underskirts to give them volume. In the 1950s, short dresses were considered appropriate only for informal weddings.

No matter what the length of the bride's dress or formality of the wedding, most bridesmaids wore short ballerina-length gowns. One popular style had a wide portrait neckline, slightly off the shoulder, with cap sleeves. Bridesmaids often wore headpieces of small circlets with face veils or the ever-popular picture hats. They carried small, round, nosegay-style bouquets and typically

Some 1950s wedding gowns came in a variety of colors besides white, including pale pink, yellow, and blue.

wore short gloves, sometimes in colors that matched their dresses. Shoes were sometimes dyed to match as well.

The pastel-colored gowns first advertised in 1946 became a minor trend in the 1950s, promoted as alternatives for older brides and for second weddings. Champagne pink (sometimes called "blush") was a favorite, as pink was a trendy color in both men's and women's clothing in the early 1950s.

Another popular way for brides to introduce color, especially effective at informal weddings, was to wear a white or ivory dress with a hat, gloves, and shoes of a second color. The bridesmaids would wear this second color as their primary shade.

POPULAR MUSICIANS OF THE 1950S

Paul Anka
Count Basie
Harry Belafonte
Tony Bennett
Les Brown
Ray Charles
Rosemary Clooney
Nat "King" Cole
Bing Crosby
Vic Damone
Sammy Davis Jr.
Doris Day
Fats Domino
Billy Eckstine
Duke Ellington
The Everly Brothers
Ella Fitzgerald
Bill Haley and the Comets
Phil Harris
Buddy Holly
Sammy Kaye
Stan Kenton
Frankie Laine
Mario Lanza
Peggy Lee
Jerry Lee Lewis
Little Richard
Julie London
Frankie Lyman and
   the Teenagers
Dean Martin
Johnny Mathis
The Mills Brothers
Patti Page
The Penguins
The Platters
Elvis Presley
Frank Sinatra
Jo Stafford
Sarah Vaughan

POPULAR SONGS OF THE 1950S

"All I Have to Do Is Dream"
"All Shook Up"
"All the Way"
"April Love"
"Because of You"
"Blueberry Hill"
"Cara Mia"
"Chances Are"
"Chanson d'Amour"
"Come Fly with Me"
"Come On-a-My House"
"Diana"
"Earth Angel"
"Fever"
"The Great Pretender"
"Hello, Young Lovers"
"Hey There"
"Hold Me, Thrill Me, Kiss Me"
"How High the Moon"
"It's So Nice to Have a Man
   Around the House"
"I've Got a Woman"
"Love and Marriage"
"Love Is a Many-Splendored Thing"
"Love Letters in the Sand"
"Love Me Tender"

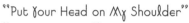
Courtesy of Capitol Records

"Lover"
"Misty"
"Moments to
   Remember"
"Mona Lisa"
"Only You"
"On the Street
   Where You
   Live"
"Put Your Head on My Shoulder"
"Que Será, Será"
"Rag Mop"
"Rags to Riches"
"Secret Love"
"September in the Rain"
"Stranger in Paradise"
"Teach Me Tonight"
"Tennessee Waltz"
"That's Amore"
"Three Coins in the Fountain"
"Till I Waltz Again with You"
"Too Young"
"Twilight Time"
"Unchained Melody"
"Unforgettable"
"Vaya con Dios"
"Volare"
"Whole Lot of Shakin' Going On"
"Why Do Fools Fall in Love?"
"With a Song in My Heart"
"You Go to My Head"
"Young at Heart"

First Things First: Thinking Thematically

C
H
A
P
T
E
R

THREE

ow that you've had a chance to browse through the past, it's time to narrow your focus to a specific era and decide if you want to apply a thematic concept for your wedding. A theme helps tie together the many disparate elements of a wedding into a cohesive event that carries your own style.

If you know which eras appeal to you, then you're already one big step ahead. If you're not sure where to start, this chapter has some exercises to help you narrow down the best potential vintage eras or themes, based on your personal interests and history.

DISCOVER WHAT'S MEANINGFUL TO YOU

ou and your fiancé should think about what has been important to your families over the past several generations. Talk to elder relatives about the times in which they lived, what they did for a living, what they did for fun, what was important in their lives. Take a look at their wedding pictures and browse through any old scrapbooks, yearbooks, and photo albums. See if you can make a connection between meaningful elements of your past family history and what's important to you today.

Think about the old places and things you love as adults—and perhaps loved when you were kids. Maybe it's the art deco hotel you pass each day on the way to work or the automobile museum in the next town. Maybe you always loved the carousel in the park. Here's a list of questions that might help you in your walk down memory lane:

- Do you collect anything? What period pieces decorate your home?
- What kind of old music makes you want to dance?
- Which are your favorite museums or museum exhibits?
- Do you have any favorite vintage buildings or parks?
- What are your favorite old plays, movies, and TV shows?
- Where did you vacation when you were growing up?
- As a child, what were your favorite things to do? Where did you like to play, and what places did you like to visit?
- Are there any family heirloom wedding gowns in the attic?
- Do you have any family mementos? What is the history behind them?

FROM CONCEPT TO COMPLETION

ere's a hypothetical example of how a theme is conceived and carried out using the exercise we just went through. Say you live in Northern California. One of your fiancé's proudest possessions is the railroad watch left to him by his great-grandfather, a train conductor in the 1930s. The golden age of rail travel has always held a special fascination for you, plus you both share a love of movies from the golden age of Hollywood.

Based on all of this, you decide to have a 1930s-style Art Deco reception in a vintage dining car on the Napa Valley wine train, following a short wedding ceremony at one of the more picturesque area wineries. You carry out the

Leah Slyder Vass is shown standing with her grandmother Katherine W. Reese, who was married in an elegant dress in 1939 (shown at right).

The silk gown consists of a redingote (a removable coat) with a cathedral-length train, worn over a bias-cut dress. Both women were delighted when the gown fit and flattered Leah perfectly, right from the attic. (Photo: Laurie Gordon)

theme by hiring a graphic designer to create a special invitation: authentic-looking train tickets inside a 1930s-style travel brochure. You hire an acoustic jazz trio to play 1930s music for atmosphere. At the reception, the two of you look elegant in your early 1930s wedding clothing—and your groom, of course, wears his great-grandfather's railroad watch. You encourage your guests to dress in period attire, and some of them do. At the table, each guest receives a wedding favor—in this case a leather luggage tag embossed with the same 1930s railroad graphics as on your invitation.

In this example, the watch, trains, and Hollywood glamour all led straight to the 1930s, and once that was decided, it was easier to find the ideal location, invitation ideas, clothing, entertainment, and other details to successfully—and tastefully—carry out the theme.

WHAT WAS HOT, DECADE BY DECADE

our wedding is the perfect opportunity to indulge your creative and romantic fantasies about another time. In this chapter we've put together a list that might help in selecting a theme.

This list contains examples of key design movements, decorating trends, arts and entertainment events and venues, travel destinations, and other miscellaneous topics from the 1910s to the 1950s. We've obviously emphasized fun and romance, but the list is by no means exhaustive. For more detailed information on each decade, or on the events and trends listed here, we suggest looking in the Americana section within the reference area of the largest library near you. Several good resources include *The Columbia Chronicles of American Life, 1910–1992,* which provides a year-by-year assessment of American popular culture and history; and the Time/Life series *This Fabulous Century,* which provides a pictorial review of the twentieth century's historical highlights and cultural trends.

As part of your research, don't forget to watch classic movies to give you a sense of period fashion and entertainment. Musicals with nightclub or hotel scenes are good for idea generation, especially when you're thinking about reception settings and decor. We've listed just a few films, film stars, and film categories as a place to start, but again, we suggest you take a trip to the library for reference books with pictures and synopses of the best films of the twentieth century.

HOT TOPICS, TRENDS, AND DIVERSIONS

The 1910s

Luxury ocean liners; cruises to Europe
Art Nouveau period design
Arts & Crafts period design
Frank Lloyd Wright
Tiffany lamps, French art glass
Panama Pacific Exposition, San Francisco
Sumptuous gardens and outdoor parties
Wicker, palms, and ferns in the garden
Vaudeville; the *Ziegfeld Follies*
Coney Island/amusement parks
Early silent films (Pickford, Fairbanks)
Sergei Diaghilev's Ballets Russe and its costumes
Isadora Duncan and modern dance
Early airplanes and dirigibles

The 1920s

Paris literary and arts scene
Paris Decorative Arts Exposition of 1925, French Art Deco
Abstract-modern art; cubism
Chinese chic (mah-jongg, kimono sleeves on dresses, Oriental rugs, rich jewel tones, lacquered furnishings)
Mediterranean influence (the tango, Mediterranean revival architecture)
Prohibition and speakeasies

Flapper and jazz culture

New York literary scene; the Algonquin Round Table; *The New Yorker; Vanity Fair*

Broadway revues and musical comedy

The heyday of "Tin Pan Alley"; the brothers Gershwin; Irving Berlin

The Great Gatsby

Silent film glamour (Cecil B. De Mille's extravaganzas, Gloria Swanson, Rudolph Valentino)

The opening of King Tut's tomb, Egyptian decorative elements

Charles Lindbergh's transatlantic crossing (and aviation culture in general)

Wintering in Florida and Hawaii

Touring America by automobile; staying at "motor courts"

Mystery novels

The 1930s

The end of Prohibition

Harlem nightclubs and the Lindy hop

Big band music and culture

New York skyscrapers

Works Progress Administration (WPA) buildings (1930s-built train stations, post offices, public buildings)

Luxury train travel

Streamlined moderne design

The *Normandie* and the *Queen Mary*

Elegant dinner/dance nightclubs; café society; elaborate floor shows

Fred Astaire movies, especially the RKO films (Art Deco movie sets galore)

Gone With the Wind

Hollywood glamour (Greta Garbo, Jean Harlow, Joan Crawford, Clark Gable)

Busby Berkeley musicals; chorus girls

Miami Beach vacations

Cabaret-style nightclubs

Radio City Music Hall

World's Fairs in Chicago (1933–34), New York (1939–40), and San Francisco
(1939–40)
Classic radio shows
Early commercial air travel (the *China Clipper*)

The 1940s

Patriotism (USO dances, war bond drives)
Big band culture, continued, featuring important vocalists (Frank Sinatra, Ella
Fitzgerald)
Pulp novels and magazines
Pinups and calendar girls
Apollo Theater
Jump blues music (Louis Jordan, Wynonie Harris, Jimmie Lunceford)
Hawaiian/South Pacific/Tiki style (bamboo, rattan, palm trees, tropical print
clothing)
Latino-tropical nightclubs and style (Havana, Miami, New York)
Latino-tropical stars (Xavier Cugat, Desi Arnaz, Carmen Miranda, Don
Ameche)
Betty Grable musicals
Film noir
Casablanca
Humphrey Bogart and Lauren Bacall
Katharine Hepburn and Spencer Tracy
Classic radio shows
Expanded commercial air travel

The 1950s

Anything French (ballet, poodles, berets, Eiffel tower, *Gigi, April in Paris,*
Parisian fashion)
Audrey Hepburn, especially in *Sabrina* and *Roman Holiday*
"Pixieish" stars (Leslie Caron, Audrey Hepburn, Shirley MacLaine, Debbie
Reynolds)
TV shows (*I Love Lucy, American Bandstand*, quiz shows)

Sex bombshell movie stars (Marilyn Monroe, Jayne Mansfield, Brigitte Bardot,
   Sophia Loren)
Diner culture
Madison Avenue advertising
Big American cars with fins
Patio cookouts
Lounge culture (the Rat Pack, Las Vegas)
Cocktail parties with martinis, Manhattans, canapés, and hors d'oeuvres
Early rock 'n' roll culture
"Atomic age" abstract graphics
Abstract art–inspired home furnishings and accessories
Googie (Los Angeles coffee shop) architecture
First commercial jet aircraft
The space race; *Sputnik*

FIRST IMPRESSIONS:
THE INVITATION

Engraved invitations are as much a part of wedding tradition as the bridal veil itself. Announcements and invitations should always be engraved to be correct.
   —MARJORIE BINFORD WOODS, *YOUR WEDDING: HOW TO PLAN AND ENJOY IT,* 1942

e've come a long way since the time when wedding invitations had to be engraved in black on white or ecru paper to be "correct." While engraved invitations are still the choice of many vintage-inspired couples, others are circumventing tradition for the sake of creative impact.

"The people we work with have looked in all the catalogs at the stationery stores and found nothing that represents who they are or what they're trying

Monica Christie and Harry Johnson wanted an invitation based on the famous VJ-Day photograph from Life *magazine. Rock Scissor Paper developed a vintage scrapbook–style invitation that included a before-and-after surprise.*

Get ready to take a step back in time
to the days when Bogey was King
and Big Bands played Swing

Monica Carla Christie
and
Harry Isaac Johnson, III

together with their parents
invite you to celebrate their wedding
in 1940's fashion

Sunday, September 13, 1998
5 o'clock

Our Lady of Mount Carmel Church
Santa Barbara, California

Dining, Dancing & Gaming to follow

Military or civilian dress of
the era encouraged

to do," says Susie Bauer of the Los Angeles design firm Rock Scissor Paper. She and her sister Heidi specialize in nontraditional wedding and party invitations inspired by the past. "Our customers don't want the typical 'storybook' weddings," says Bauer. "Because they aren't bound to tradition, they are free to express themselves in creative ways."

Most of the time, she says, this means basing a vision on such things as old movies, music, dance, personal collections, vintage clothing, pop culture, photography, or art. "They want a celebration that reflects their interests and is so fabulous that it blows everyone away. The invitation needs to convey that excitement."

An unusual invitation piques the interest of everyone who is invited, even if they live far away. "We hear it all the time. Guests the couple thought would never travel to the wedding walk up to them and say, 'How could I pass this up?' " says Bauer.

Deborah Miller Burke & Robert Wallace Hoye
present

Till Death Do Us Part

A HIGH MOON PRODUCTION

Deborah Burke and Robert Hoye staged a murder mystery at their 1912-era wedding and reception. Keeping with the theme of the evening, Burke designed a wedding invitation in the style of a vintage theater program.

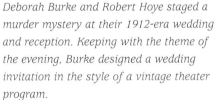

Mrs. Concetto Anthony Ambra
requests the honour of your presence
at the marriage of her daughter
Marilyn Janice
to
Mr. Nelson Victor Thorpe
Saturday, the tenth of April
Nineteen hundred and ninety-nine
at half after two o'clock Nuptial Mass

Saint Margaret Mary Church
Oakland, California

Nelson and Marilyn Thorpe chose a traditional engraved invitation for their 1930s period wedding.

(Photo: Laurie Gordon)

THE FORMAL ELEGANCE OF
COPPER PLATE ENGRAVING

Traditional wedding invitations have looked about the same for more than a century, and Vintage-loving couples who want formality, historical accuracy, or simply like the timeless, sophisticated look of engraved invitations still choose them today. And even though alternative printing techniques such as thermography or laser printing can mimic the look of engraving at lower prices, there's no substitute for the original to exude formal elegance and style.

Vintage etiquette advisers recommend that wedding invitations be

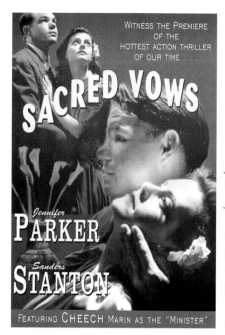

Jennifer Parker and Sanders Stanton designed this 1940s-style movie poster for their wedding invitation. The ceremony was held on Treasure Island near San Francisco and was officiated by actor and comedian Cheech Marin, who is a co-worker of Parker's. The invitation encouraged guests to dress in 1940s-style attire, and to the couple's delight, most of them did.

The Crane Company of Massachusetts has been printing engraved wedding invitations since 1801 and is still the leader in formal copper plate engraving. But even if Crane's techniques are authentically vintage, this venerable company has now gone high-tech, providing brides with a convenient resource: an online blue book of guidelines for wedding invitations.

Among the topics included are the following:

- Etiquette for all wedding invitations, announcements, and correspondence
- How to choose wedding papers, ink colors, and lettering styles
- How to handle new and unusual circumstances
- The anatomy of a wedding invitation—the significance of each and every line and enclosure card

Browse or search the *Crane's Online Wedding Blue Book* at www.crane.com/social/weddings/wedding-blue-book

engraved in black, on the first page of a double sheet of pearl white or ecru white forty-pound paper. If you have a family coat of arms, crest, or shield, emboss it on the invitation instead of die-stamping it.

Use two envelopes but don't seal the inside one; insert it into the outer envelope so that the front faces the flap. And what about that little shred of tissue paper that covers the engraving? This was originally used so that the ink wouldn't rub off on another part of the invitation. Tissue or not? Our etiquette mistresses disagree on this one: Emily Post says take it out, Amy Vanderbilt says leave it in. We'll leave this critical decision up to you.

WITH THIS RING . . .

iamonds may be forever, but they weren't always the coveted wedding jewels that they are today. This tradition essentially got its start in 1866, when an enormous diamond mine was discovered in South Africa by the De Beers mining company. De Beers lost no time promoting its

"Diamonds are Trumps" by Will Grefe, 1909.

newly found gems to the society elite. And as they had gained (and still maintain) a near monopoly on the diamond market, De Beers positioned the gems as rare and exclusive—with price tags to match. It worked. By the turn of the twentieth century, every fashionable woman had to have at least one of these girls' best friends as the glittering centerpiece of her wedding ring.

Diamonds got another boost when gem cutters developed more mathematically accurate methods of faceting stones. When cut in these new ways, diamonds sparkled brighter because they reflected more light. The first European-cut diamonds appeared about 1900, replacing the then traditional mine cut. And the European cut was eclipsed in the 1920s by an even more precise method called the brilliant cut, which is the faceting we see most often today.

The filigree ring was the hot design trend for wedding rings made between 1900 and the 1920s, named for the lacelike look of the intricate cutwork in the white gold or platinum. Using flowing motifs from the Victorian, Art Nouveau, and early French Art Deco periods, jewelers designed ornate wedding rings that were a delicate and flattering complement to the lace, beads, silk, and feathers worn by the well-heeled women of the Jazz Age.

AN ENDURING TRADITION, DRIVEN BY MARKETING

You might be surprised to learn that the matching engagement and wedding ring sets we take for granted today are a twentieth-century phenomenon. In fact, they are the result of yet another clever marketing strategy. Up until 1930 these wedding sets didn't exist. The diamond filigree ring was considered to be the wedding ring and was sometimes the only ring the bride received. If a suitor gave an engagement ring to his bride-to-be, she wore it on her other hand after the wedding, as the filigree ring wasn't shaped in a way to allow a second ring to fit on the same finger.

But the jewelry industry wanted to sell more diamonds, so they devised a strategy to sell two rings to every couple. First they suggested that a woman

A swanky hotel room in New York cost $2.50, a complete dinner $1.50, and a brand-new Maxwell roadster was $580.00 in November 1916, when Boston jeweler Jason Weiler & Son ran an ad in the Saturday Evening Post for this diamond filigree ring, "made of all platinum, richly carved and pierced in the new lace work effect. $205.00."

should wear a "guard ring" on the same finger as her diamond solitaire wedding ring, as a means to protect it from harm and keep it from falling off. The wedding and guard rings came in a matching set, and of course, the guard ring sported several diamonds. When this idea didn't catch on with consumers, the jewelers tried a new tack: they began promoting the solitaire diamond ring as the engagement ring, "to be worn as a symbol of love before the wedding."

The guard ring now became the wedding ring, to be given at the ceremony and placed on the bride's left ring finger, closest to her heart. These new romantic raisons d'être for matching wedding and engagement rings scored big with women. This clever marketing campaign signaled the beginning of what has now become a standard wedding tradition, much to the dismay of budget-minded grooms everywhere.

THE PRICE OF PROGRESS: HANDCRAFTED RINGS NEARLY DISAPPEAR

By 1930, consumer enthusiasm for the aesthetic simplicity of streamline moderne meant that the ornate filigree rings, with their flowery motifs, were now considered old-fashioned. Jewelers began to offer more simplified settings, featuring diamonds that came in exciting new shapes, such as emerald, pear, and marquise. Brides continued to prefer platinum and white gold settings, as the stark whiteness of these metals blended well with the brilliance of the diamonds. But when World War II broke out, platinum temporarily disappeared from the marketplace, as it was needed for the war effort.

After the war was over, the price of gold soared to a record $30 per ounce, causing jewelers to seek out more cost-effective manufacturing methods to keep prices in line. They accomplished this by shifting away from the traditional method of ring making—a labor-intensive process called die striking—in favor of a more expedient but cruder process called lost-wax casting, in which a precious metal is poured into a mold.

It's not difficult to see why die striking was more expensive. To die-strike a ring, a craftsman places two halves of a negative impression of a ring, or a "die," into a device consisting of an anvil and a five-hundred-pound drop hammer, mounted eighteen feet above the anvil. He then places a sheet of gold or platinum on top of the anvil and releases the hammer, causing the die to strike the metal at sixty thousand pounds per square inch. This stamps out the individual ring sections, which the jeweler trims and solders together. A ring may need from four to fifteen separate dies, depending on the complexity of the style. To finish the ring, craftsmen hand-engrave any leaves, flowers, or trim with special saws and tools, carefully cutting out the filigree work to create a delicate lacelike look. This precise detailing can take several weeks to complete.

With lost-wax casting, manufacturers could make rings faster and cheaper, but they sacrificed many of the wonderful details that were possible only with the die-struck method, as well as the sheer strength of the rings created this way. By the end of the 1940s, most wedding sets were cast, and brides selected rings made in the newly fashionable yellow gold, a preference that continued for the rest of the twentieth century. The cast ring mountings of the 1950s and beyond were far less ornate, although some still featured decorative settings for the stones, including raised areas and simple piercings along the sides of the rings. But the designs grew to be even simpler in later years, as the focal point of the wedding set became the diamonds—both in size and in quantity.

BUYING A VINTAGE RING

If you want an authentic vintage wedding or engagement ring, you're not alone. The demand for quality vintage wedding jewelry has never been greater. The best places to find these rings are jewelry stores and antiques shops that specialize in estate jewelry. But these days you can shop for vintage wedding rings even from the comfort of home, on Internet e-commerce and auction sites.

The many reasons for owning a vintage ring are obvious, but do keep a few important things in mind when shopping: After fifty to seventy years of wear, some old rings have hidden damage, including loose mountings.

Examine rings carefully under a strong magnifying lens for signs of wear. Make sure the prongs hold the gemstone securely in place. Keep in mind that white and yellow gold are softer than platinum and that cast rings are weaker than die-struck rings. Be sure to ask the jeweler or antiques dealer how the ring was made. Most estate jewelers will know the difference between die-struck and cast rings; most antiques dealers will not. Some estate jewelers will guarantee their mountings; the average antiques shop will not.

If the ring doesn't fit, understand that some vintage rings can be resized, but many others can't. An old ring may also be set with mine-cut or European-cut diamonds, which won't sparkle as much as brilliant-cut stones. The diamonds may also be smaller, as solitaires less than one carat were common. There also may be visible imperfections in the stones. If you want to mount a larger stone or one of a different shape, you might be out of luck, as older rings often can't be retrofit properly.

A SMART ALTERNATIVE: VINTAGE REPRODUCTION RINGS

A practical alternative is to consider getting a brand-new wedding ring in a vintage style, made by one of the handful of companies in the United States that still create jewelry the old-fashioned way. One such jeweler is Antique Timepieces of San Anselmo, California, now in their third generation of hand-crafting antique-style rings in the die-struck manufacturing process. Using French tools from the turn of the century and dies made from original rings of the 1900s–1930s, they custom-craft jewelry from a wide variety of vintage designs, made in the bride's choice of white gold, yellow gold, or platinum, with her stone of choice, and sized to fit her finger. Because the rings are handcrafted, they take about four to five weeks to finish. "They don't just look like antiques, they are made exactly as the antique rings were," says jeweler Drew McEachern.

If you see new filigree-style rings for sale in a jewelry shop, be cautious—McEachern warns that some jewelers are making molds from the die-struck antique rings, and then casting them with molten gold. The result is an inferior facsimile of the original, in terms of both detail and the strength of the ring. "You can see the difference when you examine these rings under a magnifying glass, as the engravings and piercings look crude by comparison," McEachern says. "It's less expensive to buy rings this way than to have them die-struck, but the quality is also much lower."

Outfitting the Wedding Party

Finding the Perfect Vintage Wedding Gown

It's more practical to save the veil for future generations than the dress. . . . Think of the bride of the twenties with her knee-length gown she thought her granddaughter would be able to wear!

—AMY VANDERBILT, 1952

t might be a bit late to dress this bride's granddaughter, but it's likely that her great-granddaughter would jump at the chance to don a 1920s wedding gown today, despite what Amy Vanderbilt thought in 1952. Vanderbilt never would have dreamed that brides of the future would be clamoring for gowns from the past, but they are, in record numbers. Stylish vintage gowns in wearable condition from the 1910s to the 1950s sell for many hundreds of dollars today. If you inherited a wedding gown—and if it fits and flatters you—you're a lucky bride. If not, you're still in luck, because

Lisa Hewitt Koester in full
1920s-style bridal regalia.

(Photo: Laurie Gordon)

we can tell you how and where to buy a vintage wedding gown or how to get a new one made in a vintage style.

GOWN SHOPPING: ON-LINE AND OFF-LINE

t used to take a lot of legwork to find a great old wedding gown. You had to comb through antique clothing shops and scour vintage cloth-ing expos, sometimes for months, until you found a dress that was

Fashion Service pattern brochure, 1930s.

just the era you wanted, that was in good shape, and that fit and flattered you.

You should still look for a gown at shops and shows, but now you have another convenient option: the World Wide Web. At any given e-moment, you can find scores of vintage wedding gowns and accessories for sale, from any decade, in all shapes and sizes.

The Web saves you shopping time and shoe leather because you can browse through a wide selection without ever leaving home. But it can be a bit challenging to buy vintage clothing sight unseen. To help you find the best gown possible and avoid the biggest pitfalls, we spoke with a few seasoned professionals who offered their advice.

MEASURE FOR SUCCESS

auren Lavonne Pritchett owns the Honolulu-based Gulden & Brown Antique and Vintage Wedding Gowns and also sells vintage dresses to customers around the world from her Web site. Pritchett says that the most important thing to do when shopping for a vintage gown is to take your measurements ahead of time and bring the tape measure with you when you try on gowns. "This will help you narrow your choices to the dresses that will fit, or can be altered to fit, whether you're shopping at a store in person or over the Internet," says Pritchett.

Deborah Burke of www.antiqueweddings.com also stresses the importance of measuring yourself and of analyzing your body shape to predetermine which dresses will work best with your figure. Burke says that most women look fine in gowns from the 1910s, 1940s, and 1950s, but the styles from 1920s and 1930s are a bit more difficult to wear. "The 1920s look requires a flatter bustline and narrow hips to carry off the dropped waists," she says, "and the form-fitting 1930s bias-cut gowns tend to look best on women who are somewhat slender and evenly proportioned."

WORKING WITH THE PROS

ritchett stresses the importance of working with knowledgeable vintage clothing dealers who can accurately report the size and condition of clothes. "Good clothing dealers will disclose every flaw a garment has, even if it means losing a sale," she says. Most vintage gowns have been worn at least once, so they'll normally have some minor damage, Pritchett told us. So the idea is to find a dress that's in wearable condition with as few problems as possible or with minor damage that can be repaired.

A reputable dealer will allow you a few days (normally from two to five) to gently and carefully try on the dress, wearing gloves to keep it clean, and

GETTING IT ALL ON TAPE

Vintage clothing expert Lauren Lavonne Pritchett recommends that brides jot down these measurements before shopping:

1. Bust. Keeping the tape measure straight, measure around the fullest part of your bust at the widest part of the back. Be sure not to slouch. Write this measurement down.
2. Waist. Wrap the tape measure around your waist. Exhale, letting the tape settle at your natural waistline. Do not pull it tight. You should be able to sit comfortably with the tape measure in place. If not, relax the tape a bit to allow for "wearing ease." For a close-fitting garment, wearing ease can run up to an inch extra at the waist and two inches extra at the hip and the bust. It's better to overestimate slightly and add wearing ease to your measurements, especially if you are planning an active day.
3. Hips. Measure around the fullest part of your hip, above the uppermost thigh, approximately seven to nine inches below the waist.
4. Arms. don't forget to measure the circumference at the tops of your arms if you want a short-sleeved or sleeveless gown.

While you've got the tape measure handy, vintage clothing dealer Deborah Burke suggests including these measurements as well:

5. Back. Measure across your upper back, across your shoulder blades from armpit to armpit.
6. Rib cage. If you want a gown with an Empire waist, measure around your rib cage, just under your bustline.
7. Height, without shoes.

Even with accurate measurements, Pritchett advises that your gown may need some minor alterations for it to fit just right. She suggests that you budget an extra $100 or so for a last-minute set of nips and tucks.

send it back if it doesn't fit or flatter you. Ask about the return policy beforehand, and make sure you clearly understand it and agree to its terms and conditions before paying any money. If there's no reasonable return policy, beware.

Buying a vintage gown can be difficult at a distance, but some Internet-based dealers provide a level of service above and beyond what you'll find in most brick-and-mortar storefronts. Deborah Burke's longtime love affair with vintage clothing is clearly reflected in the hundreds of meticulously photographed garments in her Web storefront, which features not only an extensive selection of vintage wedding dresses from almost every era, but also a wide assortment of couture and museum-quality gowns and accessories.

"I want to talk to my brides," Burke says. "You won't find any of that 'drop it in the cart and pay' mentality here. I want to make sure they've taken a tape measure out and measured themselves; that they know how to judge the clothing and how to try it on; and that they understand which undergarments and accessories to wear with the gowns."

Burke has earned the loyalty of her customers by taking the time to assist and educate them, as evidenced by the many referrals and repeat business she's gotten over the years. "I've had very few returns, and I think that one of the reasons for this is the personal touch," she says. "I really enjoy this, and I guess it comes across to people. My experiences of working over the Internet have just been fabulous."

Donna Barr of A Vintage Wedding takes an additional step in her Internet storefront. Once a bride picks out a gown, Barr adjusts a dress form in her studio to duplicate her measurements and height. "In a sense, we 'try the dress on' the customer before we send it out," Barr says. "We want to make sure up front that it will fit." She agrees with the other dealers that doing business over the Internet has gone smoother than she originally thought it would. "We do get returns sometimes, because a gown has to suit somebody. But we really don't get as many gowns back as we expected we would. People have been very happy with the process."

BUYING FROM AUCTION WEB SITES

n-line auction sites present another opportunity for gown shopping—along with a set of unique challenges. A simple search on a site such as eBay for "vintage (or antique, or old) wedding dress (or gown)" will turn up a dozen or more wedding gowns at any given time. It's possible to get an excellent vintage dress at a bargain, but it's also possible to end up with an unwearable, overpriced, or misrepresented garment. We cite these recent examples of gowns up for auction:

- ◉ A gown represented as "antique" (it was obviously from the 1980s), with a minimum asking bid of $500. (No bids; a clear misrepresentation)
- ◉ A lovely satin early 1940s gown, good condition report, with no reserve. ($25 bid, with two days left; a potential bargain)
- ◉ A 1930s-era dress represented as a 1910s dress, with no front view, no condition report, a $300 suggested opening price, and a hidden reserve. (No bids; possibly an honest mistake, but a careless, overpriced misrepresentation)
- ◉ A stunning late 1930s lace and rayon satin formal wedding gown, with sweetheart neckline, beaded bodice, long draped sleeves, headpiece and veil, and two hand-tinted photos of the original bride. Includes detailed measurements and a condition report. ($235 final price—a bargain)

Some misrepresentations on auction sites are honest mistakes. Many sellers (and even some antiques dealers) aren't familiar enough with fashion to date a dress, confirm its condition, or accurately describe its fabric or lace. Most don't know how to measure the dress or what flaws they should report. As the buyer, you need to know if something will fit, is fairly clean, will look good, and will not fall apart at the altar. But sometimes all you have to go on is a fuzzy picture and a vague description.

Here's a perfect example of what could happen: You win the bid on a great-looking vintage wedding dress and send payment. Two weeks later you open the shipping box and find a visible grease stain on the bodice. This is a legitimate reason for returning it, right? The seller says nope . . . you saw the picture. You *did* see the picture (it was small, dark, and fuzzy), and you assumed the stain was a shadow. Your dry cleaner says that he can't budge the stain from the fabric. Guess what? You've just bought yourself an unwearable wedding dress.

If you shop for a wedding gown on an auction Web site, you're rolling the dice. Stack the odds in your favor by following our tips for auction shopping (see box). Remember, a bargain's not a bargain if it hangs unworn in your closet.

Alexandra Garner tries on vintage gowns at Shadows in San Anselmo, California.

(Photo: Laurie Gordon)

INSPECTING A DRESS FOR FLAWS

hether you're buying a gown on the Internet or shopping for a dress the old-fashioned way, it's important to know how to inspect a gown for structural soundness and how to evaluate its flaws.

Fabric is not impervious to age, and it's only a matter of time before the elements begin to take their toll. The amount of deterioration in a garment depends on such things as the type of fabric, the frequency of wear, how well or poorly the item was cared for, whether it was exposed to light and other elements over time, whether it was hung on a hanger or heirloom boxed, if it was ever dry-cleaned, and so on. Consequently you can sometimes find dresses from the 1950s that are falling apart and dresses from the 1910s that look like new. Generally speaking, the old silk wedding

CAVEAT EMPTOR-DOT-COM

Here are some important things to do when bidding on a vintage wedding gown on an auction Web site:

- Look at the seller's feedback record. Don't bid on the dress if you see any complaints about misrepresentations, refusal to honor returns, or evidence of a "prickly" personality.
- If the seller doesn't provide enough details about the dress, ask for more. Offer to call on the phone. If you get no response or a vague answer, or if the seller seems annoyed by your questions, *don't* bid on the dress.
- If the pictures are unclear, or if they don't show the front *and* back of the dress, ask to see others. Reputable sellers will gladly provide these if you're a serious buyer. Pictures should include close-ups of any serious flaws.
- Get a detailed inventory of flaws, in writing. Don't buy dresses with stains in visible areas or dresses advertised as "needs cleaning." Don't believe anyone who says that a stain will "definitely" come out. Accept that all dresses will have some degree of wear and tear that you'll have to fix or wear as is. Beware of buying any silk gowns made prior to the 1950s, as the fabric disintegrates with age.
- Find out if the seller has a return policy—but don't count on it. Most honor returns only if an item was misrepresented. Remember that it's not misrepresentation if a dress doesn't fit or flatter you, if you find something better later, or if you get buyer's remorse. If you hate the dress after you buy it, resell it yourself. You may even get more than you paid for it!
- Pay by credit card if you can. If you have a problem with the dress and the seller won't take it back, turn to the credit card company for help.
- If you can't use a credit card, use the auction site's escrow service to handle the transaction. Don't skimp on the modest amount this will cost you—it's cheap insurance.

dresses—often the most beautiful of all—are the fastest to deteriorate, with most showing evidence of progressive fabric failure after just forty years or so. Fortunately, the rayon gowns so popular from the 1930s forward are holding up very well.

Most vintage wedding gowns were worn at least once—some more vigorously than others. By nature, wedding gowns are cumbersome and unwieldy to wear in the best of circumstances. It's easy for guests or your groom to step on your train or hem or for you to brush against a dirty snowbank or inadvertently dip a bit of your lacy sleeve into the crème brûlée. Not only that, but wedding days are always stressful, and wedding dresses are hot to wear. Stress and heat result in perspiration.

It's logical to assume, then, that any gown worn once will have a fair

DAMAGE CONTROL

*W*hen you are evaluating a vintage gown, it helps to understand the difference between things that you should overlook, things that you can fix, and things that make a dress unwearable.

EASY TO REPAIR

Rusted buttons
Ripped trains
Torn undernetting
Missing beads
Missing or damaged pearls and buttons
Broken zippers
Tears on seams
Some pulls in the fabric
Minor lace tears

USUALLY NOT REPAIRABLE

Split or "shattered" silk (fabric deterioration)
Dry rot in fabric or lace (fabric is dry and brittle)
Badly torn lace
Rust stains
Visible stains or dirt in conspicuous places
Tears, holes, or burns in visible places
Visible underarm stains

ACCEPT THESE MINOR DEFECTS AS IS

Hem dirt
Water staining on the hem or train
Inconspicuous stains
Inconspicuous small holes
Minor scratches, scuffs, or pulls

amount of wear and tear. A reasonable goal is to find a dress that's a lot like your groom: structurally sound, with a reasonable number of flaws that you can live with.

The most important place to check for serious structural damage is in the bodice, especially around the shoulder and arms. "The dress hangs on the body from here, and any normal twisting and turning, plus the weight of the gown, will stress the fabric," says Lauren Pritchett. Dresses kept in closets on hangers for years may also show extra stress from hanging, especially in the shoulder and bodice area. Some dresses may become misshapen after years of hanging because the weight of the skirt stretched out the supporting fabric in the bodice.

Look closely to see if the fabric has separated or torn or if any parts of the gown feel dry or papery, possibly indicating dry rot. Inspect the armpit area for disintegration. Even dresses without noticeable armpit stains can have damage here, as perspiration acts like acid on fabric.

If the dress appears structurally sound, the next thing to check for is visible damage that detracts from the gown's appearance, such as dirt, stains, holes, and tears (see box).

TO DRY-CLEAN OR NOT?

ll gowns need pressing or steaming, but think twice before dry cleaning. The chemicals are harsh, stains may or may not come out, and some stains that were not visible to the eye can become more noticeable afterward. Pearl buttons or trim can disintegrate or discolor; beads can fall off or become loose. It's usually difficult to find someone who knows how to dry-clean vintage gowns properly, and it can be very expensive. If you decide to dry-clean a gown, consider shipping it to an expert heirloom restorer for cleaning and then have it pressed locally right before the wedding. Most reputable dry cleaners can steam-press a vintage dress.

Donna Barr says she's had good experience dry cleaning the heavy rayon satin gowns that were popular in the 1940s and 1950s. "These dresses are really quite durable," says Barr. She cautions us, however, about old chiffon, which she says is almost impossible to bring back to its original condition once it's gone dingy or gray. If you think your vintage gown is sturdy enough for dry cleaning, take it to a reputable dry cleaner who regularly works on expensive evening gowns and wedding dresses. To find a good dry cleaner, ask for a recommendation at better clothing stores or wedding gown shops.

If you need to dry-clean something older than a 1930s gown, a silk dress, or a vintage dress with a lot of trim, consider sending it to an antique gown restoration specialist. It costs more to clean a dress this way, so the gown would have to be special enough to merit the extra expense. Look on the Internet for restoration services that specialize in cleaning antique gowns (we've listed a popular one in our "Resources" directory) or ask a local museum curator whom they would recommend.

Some vintage clothing dealers will assure you that a spot will come out of a gown, but don't assume this is a certainty. See if you can negotiate the dry cleaning as part of the transaction. Ask the dealer to clean the dress first, and promise that if the stain comes out, you'll buy the dress and pay the cleaning bill. If the stain doesn't come out with cleaning (as was claimed), the dealer keeps the dress and pays for the cleaning. A reputable dealer will find this arrangement fair unless she is selling a dress "as is," in which case she'll tell you this up front and not make any promises about stain removal. Of course, be sure to make any agreements in writing. Because dry cleaning is not always an option, and to avoid the extra expense of heirloom restoration, it's usually wise to look for a vintage wedding gown that has minor damage and can be worn as is.

REMODELING AND RESTORATION

f you find a great gown that doesn't fit you quite right or has a few minor problems, find out if it can be altered or partially restored. Be sure that it's not too small—it's much more difficult and often impossible to make a gown larger, especially in the bodice. Ask an experienced tailor or seamstress for advice. In most cases you'll be able to replace or restyle sleeves, shorten hems, and remove or shorten trains.

Restoration is trickier and, in most cases, not possible if the fabric is disintegrating. But you can get creative sometimes if the dress is special enough to warrant the extra expense of remodeling. For example, if the gown has a fabulous bodice with an unwearable skirt (or vice versa), consider replacing the damaged half using a complementary kind of fabric. Obviously this would work better with some styles than with others. You and your seamstress can discuss the options.

In some cases torn lace can be replaced or patched or beads and lace can be added to cover stains or minor damage. Seamstresses at Gulden & Brown added some beading around the neckline and bodice of Suzette Prasatek's vintage gown to camouflage some light yellowing of the fabric. "The beading they added was absolutely beautiful, and it really enhanced the gown," she said.

Even the plainest wedding gown can be dressed up by adding embellishments of embroidery, beadwork, silk flowers, or lace appliqués. You'll occasionally see an example of a vintage wedding gown, usually from the 1930s or 1940s, with flowers of crystal beads and pearls that were painstakingly added by loving hands to the simple bodice more than half a century ago.

THE CROWNING GLORY

intage headpieces are easy to find at Internet storefronts and auction sites. They are often in good condition, most of the time having sustained less damage than a wedding dress. If the veil netting is torn or deteriorated, don't be too concerned, as simple netting (except for elaborate veils with lace edges, for example) is easily replaced. Watch for headpieces that have yellowed excessively or are stained from ancient glue residue. Inspect for missing beads or stones.

Be sure to wear a headpiece that is accurate to the period and style of your

An authentic 1920s headpiece made of wax orange blossoms. (Photo: Laurie Gordon)

gown. Don't mix eras. Review the headpieces we showed in chapter 2 so that you know what styles to look for. Headpieces from the 1930s and 1940s looked very similar, and these are fairly easy to find. If you want a 1920s headpiece, it will be tough to locate an authentic vintage one in good condition at a reasonable price. You might consider a reproduction 1920s bandeaux-style headpiece from San Diego's Atelier Polonaise (see "Resources"), or find a seamstress who can reproduce a 1920s headpiece, such as a wreath of silk orange blossoms. A slightly larger crown of orange blossoms with a long, simple veil is also perfect for a 1910s headpiece.

SEWING A VINTAGE-STYLE WEDDING GOWN: A PRACTICAL ALTERNATIVE

ome brides decide to sew a vintage-style gown of their own or work with a seamstress to have a dress made. Here are some situations in which a "new vintage" gown might be practical:

- You know the style and era of gown you want, but you can't find an original vintage one like it anywhere.
- You found the dress of your dreams, but it's either in unwearable condition, the wrong size, or the wrong fabric.
- You want a dress exactly like your grandmother's, except hers was lost years ago and all you have is her picture.
- You got your grandmother's dress out of the attic, but it's three sizes too small.
- You have a favorite vintage dress and want a wedding gown made in a similar style.
- You found the perfect vintage wedding dress pattern.
- You found a picture of the exact style of dress you want in an old book or magazine.
- You feel uncomfortable wearing someone else's wedding gown.

If you're a whiz at the sewing machine, you can make your own wedding dress from a pattern. Be sure to make a muslin copy first, using a dress form sized to your figure for fitting. But know that vintage wedding gown patterns are tricky to cut and difficult to sew, requiring precise manipulation of large, slippery pieces of fabric. If you haven't threaded a bobbin since home economics class, you might want to leave the dressmaking to the experts.

WORKING WITH A CLOTHING DESIGNER OR SEAMSTRESS

Theresa LaQuey designs original vintage-style clothing for clients, with much of her work devoted to wedding attire. A trained artist and pattern maker, LaQuey was hired by the Simplicity Pattern Company to design a line of vintage reproduction patterns. To date, her work for Simplicity includes a 1930s evening gown, a 1940s swing dance dress, and designs based on two of the dresses from the film *Breakfast at Tiffany's,* with more on the way.

LaQuey first meets with a client to find out what she wants, encouraging her to bring along pictures or examples of favorite vintage clothing. Based on the client's likes and dislikes as well as the shape of her body, LaQuey then creates a sketch, making recommendations about the styles and details that would work best for the client. Once the client approves the design, LaQuey creates the pattern and begins sewing a muslin sample.

Naturally, it makes sense for you to work with seamstresses or fashion designers in your part of the country. We asked LaQuey what the right dress-maker should do:

- Draw a good sketch of the garment and give it to you for approval as soon as possible after the initial consultation. Or, if you're working from a commercial pattern, she should advise whether or not it will flatter your body and make suggestions for revisions.
- Mock up the dress in muslin before cutting any fabric. LaQuey says that this is where any problems with the dress are identified and fixed. "The pattern has to be right before the pieces go together. I don't make just one muslin, either. I can run up to five if necessary. I want the client to stand in front of the mirror in a muslin dress, jumping up and down, saying, 'This is exactly what I want!' before I even touch the final fabric."
- Adhere to an agreed-upon timetable, including getting you your sketch on time, and scheduling timely fittings. She should also plan to deliver the dress at least a few weeks before your wedding, not at the last minute.
- Provide you with a clear cost estimate and a breakdown of what that entails.

As a client, you can do the following to help your seamstress do a good job:

- Give your seamstress enough time to create and sew your dress. "Even the simplest wedding gown takes thirty hours," says LaQuey. If time is short, consider working from a commercial pattern instead.

- Work way ahead of time. Your designer might have other projects due ahead of yours.
- Do a little homework first. Bring pictures. When Tonya Castleman researched her 1930s dress, she found examples by borrowing books from the library, buying old wedding photos, and looking through her grandmother's old photo albums.

Clothing designer Theresa LaQuey is shown here in the dress she created based on the wedding gown Ginger Rogers wore in the film Swing Time. *Each of LaQuey's bridesmaids also wore gowns modeled after those worn by Rogers in various films.*

(Photo: Laurie Gordon)

- Understand that you'll need multiple fittings. Be flexible, and be on time for appointments.
- Understand that this is custom work and that good craftsmanship costs money. You will have a custom gown made for about the same price as a manufactured dress, but the quality and materials of the handmade gown will almost always be superior.

Theresa LaQuey designed and stitched Lisa Hewitt's 1920s robe de style *gown, including the three hundred silk grape leaves and clusters adorning the skirt and headpiece. The grapes were a nod to the fact that Hewitt and husband Mark Koester were married in a northern California vineyard.* (Photo: Laurie Gordon)

① Don't change your mind without knowing that there's a price to pay for starting over. You'll need to compensate the seamstress for the work she's already done.

SOMETHING NEW FROM SOMETHING OLD

Many seamstresses can reproduce designs from vintage clothing samples. If you find the gown of your dreams, but it's unwearable for whatever reason, have a designer or seamstress reproduce it in a new fabric and tailor it to fit your body. You can often reuse the vintage buttons, lace, or other trim from an old gown and end up with a gorgeous vintage wedding dress, only brand new and fitting like a glove.

LaQuey cautions that sometimes a pattern or clothing you pick to reproduce may not flatter you—a dress or pattern may need revisions before it looks right. A seamstress can suggest the changes necessary for it to suit your body type.

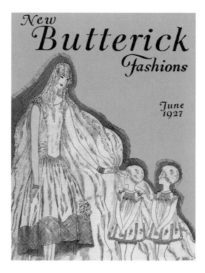

A brochure of Butterick patterns, June 1927.

VINTAGE FASHION RESEARCH, AT YOUR FINGERTIPS

Vogue and Butterick offer a research service if you need information on authentic fashions from earlier times. For a fee of $35 per hour (the first twenty minutes are free), pattern archivist Sherry Onna Handlin will dig through the books, magazines, catalogs, and old patterns in the Vogue and Butterick archives and send you information on any era back to the 1860s. The company's old patterns aren't available to consumers, but she can copy and send you pictures from pattern envelopes and catalogs. The archive is open Mondays and Thursdays, 9:30 A.M. to 4:30 P.M. eastern time. Reach Sherry by calling (212) 620-2790.

1913-Leda
Inspired by the East, this gown is
very much the fashion of the prewar
years. The feminine form is draped
to enhance curves and draw attention
to the waist, long line of the leg, hip
and ankle. The back waist is accented
with a ribbon ornament and the train is
finished with a silk tassel.
#1913-LEDABRGWN-SD
Price /995.00 (silk damask)

*Above: This beau-
tiful 1910s-style
wedding gown is
by San Diego's
Atelier Polonaise.
The back waist is
accented with a
ribbon ornament,
and the train is
finished with a silk
tassel.*

*Right: A 1940s
wedding gown
pattern by
Advance,
purchased on eBay
in 1999 for $24.*

CUSTOM VINTAGE GOWNS, FROM A CATALOG

Holly Hess and Shirley Kime create historically accurate wedding gowns in styles adapted from old fashion plates as well as from museum and private collections. Their company is Atelier Polonaise, a unique clothing studio in San Diego, where customers can select from any one of their hundred authentic gown designs, constructed from reproduction silks and lace.

If you're interested in twentieth-century styles, you can pick from a selection of gowns from the 1900s through the 1940s, as well as veils and clothing for attendants. Hess and Kime will also sew custom gowns from new or vintage patterns or will work from photos or drawings. It's not necessary to be in San Diego, either, as they regularly work with clients at great distances who pick their designs from a catalog and send in their measurements.

PATTERNS FROM THE PAST

If you look long enough, you may find an authentic vintage wedding dress pattern in good condition, in a style you like. These patterns are becoming rare, however, and command premium prices. The best places to look are at vintage clothing shows, at antique fabric expositions, and on the World Wide Web. Tonya Castleman sewed her 1930s gown from a pattern she found on the Internet auction site eBay. "I used a vintage evening dress pattern I found there as a model for my gown," she says. "I also got some great buttons that came from a 1901 wedding dress."

Castleman's example is worth noting for another important reason: Many wedding gowns made before the 1950s were modeled after the evening and formal wear of the period. So don't overlook vintage evening gown patterns—by using the right fabric and trim, you just might be able to make a great wedding dress. This fact is even more important if you're considering a 1950s wedding. The evening gowns of the 1950s have proven to be far more timeless and elegant (think Audrey Hepburn) than many of the wedding gown styles made at that time, so be sure to seek out evening wear patterns from that decade as possible choices.

NEW VINTAGE PATTERNS FROM VOGUE, BUTTERICK, AND SIMPLICITY

Here's an exciting bit of news for fans of vintage clothing: Some of the major pattern companies are realizing the demand for vintage patterns and are either reissuing old patterns or designing new ones in vintage styles. To date, we haven't seen any new retro wedding gown patterns, but several of the beautiful vintage evening gown styles can easily be adapted for weddings.

In 1998, one of the top names in clothing design, Vogue Patterns, began reissuing classic patterns from its archives in a line called Vintage Vogue. The company also reissues vintage patterns from its Butterick line, called Retro Butterick. Several patterns from each

Vintage Vogue's 1930s-style evening gown pattern.

One of the most beautiful Vintage Vogue patterns is #2241, a bias-cut evening gown, originally issued in 1931. The pattern description reads as follows: "Close-fitting, slightly flared dress, evening length, has front inset, seam detail, back shoulder bands/fold-back facings/drape/snap closing and belt. Recommended fabrics: Silk-like crepe, cut velvet and lightweight satin."

Dawn Boehmer, customer service representative for Butterick/Vogue, comments, "This is our third most popular pattern. It's gorgeous, but it can be a bit of a construction challenge, as it's all cut on the bias. So the only thing I'd suggest is to be a fairly advanced sewer, or have a seamstress make it for you. It's not a beginner's pattern."

line are released every season. According to Dawn Boehmer, customer service representative at Vogue/Butterick, "The greatest thing about this idea is that it was totally driven by our customers. The response has been so great that we have a hard time keeping the patterns on the shelves." Boehmer is on hand weekdays to provide advice and consultation to anyone who might have a question or problem when sewing any of the company's patterns.

The Simplicity Pattern Company is developing a line of vintage-inspired patterns, also in a line called Retro. This line includes Theresa LaQuey's creations as well as those of other designers. At present there are no vintage wedding gown patterns, but again, some of the evening gown styles can be adapted. For example, LaQuey's pattern for Audrey Hepburn's *Breakfast at Tiffany's* gown would make a fantastic wedding dress. Simplicity even offers a zoot suit pattern, perfect for that over-the-top 1930s or 1940s event.

WEDDING FLOWERS: OF SHOWER BOUQUETS AND LOVERS' KNOTS

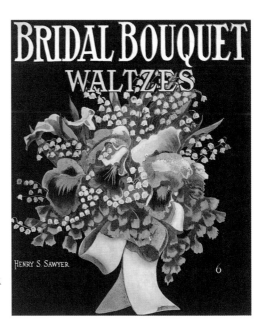

ust after the turn of the twentieth century, brides walked down the aisle carrying a new and fashionable kind of wedding bouquet. It consisted of a bundle of loosely arranged blossoms, with pendants of ribbons and greenery cascading halfway to the floor. Called the shower bouquet, it was a departure from the round, tightly formed, formal bouquets popular with brides in Victorian times.

No shower bouquet was complete without dozens of long, slender streamers of white silk ribbon tied with multiple "lovers' knots" at various places along the lengths, with little sprigs of flowers or greenery inserted into

Sheet music for a 1910s song.

A 1930s bride emerges from her car carrying an enormous shower bouquet of roses, lilies of the valley, and ferns, with yards of white silk baby ribbon tied in lovers' knots.

them. These lovers' knots are part of a forgotten wedding custom. Most everyone knows that the woman who catches the bridal bouquet will be the next to wed. But few know the second part of this tradition: If this woman unties one of the lovers' knots on the bouquet, any wish she makes at that moment will be granted.

It's not clear exactly where the trend for giant wedding bouquets originated. More than likely it was inspired by some Hollywood silent film star who carried one on screen. But however it started, sometime in the early 1920s brides began toting oversize wedding bouquets, several times larger than those carried in the 1910s. Oddly, the giant bouquets with their plentiful ribbon streamers were a well-balanced element of the typical theatrical 1920s bridal ensemble, consisting of a short wedding dress, a large, crownlike headpiece, and an enormous cathedral-length veil.

The fad for giant shower bouquets continued well into the 1930s. They still looked great, carried by Art Deco brides in their slender, bias-cut wedding gowns. In the 1940s, some brides still carried shower bouquets, but they had grown a lot smaller, and the tradition of lovers' knots started disappearing right around the beginning of World War II. After the war, the new bridal sil-

Sarah Klotz de Aguilar carries an armload of flowers, once known as a "Bernhardt bouquet."
(Photo: Laurie Gordon)

houette of tight bodices, cinched waists, and bouffant skirts was better balanced by the small, round, formal bouquets similar to the nosegays that were carried in Victorian times. After forty-five years, the shower bouquet, with its cascading lovers' knots, had become a thing of the past.

In 1905, *Home Arts and Entertainment* magazine suggested carrying a "Bernhardt bouquet," which was simply an armload of flowers and greenery. The article advised, "The more carelessly this armful is arranged the better, as though the young lady had gathered them herself." Although the article originally proposed this bouquet for bridesmaids, the Bernhardt-style armload of flowers soon became a favorite of brides—especially for informal weddings, as a smart and practical alternative to a traditional bouquet.

THE BASIC BLOOMS

Many of the flowers popular in bridal bouquets today are the same beloved blossoms that were used a hundred years ago. The wedding flowers most commonly cited in books and magazines in the first half of the twentieth century included calla lilies, cymbidium orchids, hyacinths, orange blossoms, lilies of the valley, gardenias, stephanotis, and white rosebuds.

Up until the 1950s, when brides started experimenting with color, vintage bridal bouquets were made with white flowers and greenery. Until about 1940, they also included the requisite multiple silk streamer ribbons with lovers' knots. At times, various decorative materials were added to the bouquet for dramatic effect, such as the way an occasional 1920s bride would frame hers with a ruffle of ostrich feathers.

Those striving for historical accuracy or a classic, formal vintage look might choose an all-white bouquet, and the effect of this can be striking. Imagine the elegance of a 1930s Art Deco bride in her bias-cut gown, carrying an all-gardenia shower bouquet, trimmed with variegated ivy streaming to the floor, trailing with dozens of silk ribbons.

As we're liberally throwing tradition to the wind for the sake of creativity in this book, we propose that you tailor your bridal bouquet to your theme and color palette. Think unconventionally—feel free to consider unusual flowers not normally included on the standard list of wedding favorites. Envision a bride at a tropical-theme wedding, walking down the aisle in her sarong-style gown and carrying an armload of exotic ginger, bird of paradise, antherium, and protea. Or think about an early 1940s bride, carrying a dramatic bouquet of magnolia blossoms clipped from the tree in her yard.

ORANGE BLOSSOMS: FROM DEITIES, TO ROYALTY, TO YOU

You might not think to wear orange blossoms on your wedding day, but these flowers were almost universally included on bridal gowns and headpieces in the nineteenth and early twentieth centuries. Some say that the Roman goddess Juno gave a wreath of the flowers to Jupiter on their wedding day. But Queen Victoria is best known for reviving these flowers after she wore them at her wedding in 1840.

In ancient times, orange blossoms were considered a symbol of fertility because orange trees are almost always in flower. But in staid Victorian times, fertility was out and purity was in. The fad for orange blossoms was under way, but only after they were repositioned as a symbol of virginity and beauty.

The rest of the British royal family soon picked up the trend. Princess Alice wore these flowers in her hair and around the entire circumference of her gown in 1861. And, at her marriage to the Prince of Wales in 1863, Princess Alexandra not only wore a crown of orange blossoms in her hair, but draped garland

Theresa LaQuey's wedding was in November, so she picked a palette of harvest colors for her bouquet. In addition to roses in shades of rust, peach, and cognac, she included pepper berries and sprigs from the flame vine in her backyard.

(Photo: Laurie Gordon)

after garland around her skirts in such quantities that she was chided for looking like a walking flower garden.

In the twentieth century, brides used orange blossoms with a much lighter hand, incorporating them into headpieces or pinning them to their gowns. But after World War II, these delicate and fragrant flowers fell out of favor. A 1946 edition of *The Bride's* magazine dismissed them, saying, "Gone are the times when a spray of orange blossoms made a headdress." Despite this pronouncement, some still followed the old tradition. In fact, Jacqueline Kennedy and Aristotle Onassis both wore orange blossoms in their hair when they married in 1969.

Orange blossoms, from a 1920s Florida postcard folder.

In the mid–twentieth century, Emily Post advised that second-time brides or widows should never wear orange blossoms, as they're considered a symbol of virginity. To this we simply say: Feh. Orange blossoms are a perfect addition to your vintage wedding ensemble at any age. Wear them in your hair, as part of your headpiece, or pinned to your gown. Don't be discouraged if you can't get fresh blooms—even the British royal family used wax replicas. But if you use artificial flowers, be sure to use the best silk blossoms you can find.

FLOWERS FOR THE ATTENDANTS

In years past when the bride's bouquet consisted of all-white flowers, the bridesmaids' bouquets were colorful and smaller than the bride's. Now that brides carry colorful bouquets as well, be sure that your bridesmaids' bouquets complement yours without duplicating it exactly. For garden weddings or informal ceremonies, especially in the spring or summer, it's a lovely vintage idea for bridesmaids to carry old-fashioned baskets of flowers on their arms—especially the sturdy wicker kind that look like upside-down hats with ruffled edges.

At formal weddings, the best man and the father should wear gardenias, and the groom should wear a spray from the bride's bouquet. At traditional formal weddings, the groom usually wore a sprig of lily of the valley. If you have a flower girl, she can fling petals from an upturned vintage child's hat or scoop them out of a tiny basket. Groomsmen sometimes wore carnations in earlier days, but you may choose to substitute a more elegant flower, such as a gardenia, rosebud, stephanotis, or bachelor's button. Just be sure the groom's flower is different from all the others in the party and that the best man also wears a different flower from that worn by the groom or the groomsmen.

This early 1920s bridesmaid carried a basket of flowers instead of a bouquet.

FLORAL HINTS FOR THE FRUGAL BRIDE

Some brides on a budget might look for ways to cut back on floral expenses, which can tally up fast. If you have a flower garden or flowering bushes or trees, think about how these might be used for an artistic bouquet. Deborah Burke raided her garden for the fresh tulips she and her bridesmaids carried at her 1910s-era wedding in Massachusetts. And Theresa LaQuey asked her florist to incorporate some flame vine from her garden, but it wasn't strictly because of the cost savings. LaQuey told us, "I feel that it's a good omen to use things from your own backyard on your wedding day."

Gladiolas are elegant, simple, and—best of all—inexpensive. They also come in a wide variety of colors. Buy gladiolas at bulk rate from a florist and arrange them yourself. They look great in tall vases at the ceremony or reception. To separate the stems evenly, tape green florist's tape in a grid pattern across the tops of the vases and arrange the flowers within the grid.

OUTFITTING THE GROOM AND GROOMSMEN

The bride's gown, and not the time of day, determines the formality of the wedding.

—*THE WEDDING WORK BOOK*, 1958

Nelson Thorpe adjusts his bow tie before the ceremony.

(Photo: Laurie Gordon)

he groom and his attendants take their clothing cues from the bride. If her gown has a long train, the wedding is considered formal. If her train is short, the wedding is semiformal or informal. If her gown has no train, the wedding is informal.

Once you have decided on the formality of your wedding as well as the decade, consult the chart in this chapter to find out what your groom should wear. Note that the men's attire differs slightly, depending on whether a wedding is before or after six in the evening or if it's held in the summer. The chart is organized by decade, degree of formality, season, and time of day.

Here are a few other hints for the men in the wedding:

- All the men in the wedding party should dress alike as much as possible.

CLOTHING FOR THE GROOM, BY DECADE

	INFORMAL DAY	INFORMAL EVENING
1910S	① Three-button gray or dark blue business suit; dark or white waistcoat; white shirt with rounded collar and four-in-hand or bow tie; black hose and shoes; derby hat; gray gloves. ① Summer: Dark blue or gray three-button coat with white waistcoat; white flannel trousers; white shirt with rounded collar, dark bow tie; white shoes; white gloves.	① Three-button gray or dark blue business suit; dark or white waistcoat; white shirt with rounded collar and four-in-hand or bow tie; black hose and shoes; derby hat; gray gloves. ① Summer: Dark blue or gray three-button coat with white waistcoat; white flannel trousers; white shirt, dark bow tie; white shoes and gloves.
1920S	① Gray or dark blue suit; dark or white waistcoat; white starched shirt with round collar; striped necktie or bow tie in white or black; derby or felt hat. ① Summer: Dark blue or gray coat with white flannel trousers; white shirt; dark bow tie; white shoes. ① Palm Beach suit; Panama hat. *Or* white linen suit; straw hat.	① Gray or dark blue suit; dark or white waistcoat; white starched shirt with round collar; striped necktie or bow tie in white or black; derby or felt hat. ① Summer: Dark blue or gray coat with white waistcoat; white flannel trousers; white shirt; dark bow tie; white shoes.
1930S	① Gray or dark blue double-breasted business suit; pleated and cuffed trousers; white fold collar and four-in-hand tie; black hose and shoes; felt or derby hat; gray gloves. ① Summer: Dark blue or gray coat with white flannel trousers; white shirt, dark bow tie; white shoes. *Or* Palm Beach suit; Panama hat. *Or* white linen suit; straw hat.	① Gray or dark blue double-breasted business suit; pleated and cuffed trousers; white fold collar and four-in-hand tie; black hose and shoes; felt or derby hat; gray gloves. ① Gray or dark blue coat with white flannel trousers; white shirt, dark bow tie.
1940S	① Dark blue or gray business suit; white starched shirt; four-in-hand or bow tie; black hose and shoes; felt hat. ① Summer: Palm Beach suit; Panama hat. ① White linen suit; straw hat.	① Dark blue or gray business suit; white starched shirt; four-in-hand or bow tie; black hose and shoes; felt hat. ① Gray or dark blue coat with white flannel trousers; white shirt; dark bow tie. ① Summer: White linen suit.
1950S	① Dark blue business suit; white starched shirt; four-in-hand or bow tie; black hose and shoes. ① Summer: White linen suit; straw hat. *Or* light jacket and dark trousers, or dark jacket and light trousers; white shirt; black or navy bow tie or necktie.	① Dark blue or gray business suit; white stiff shirt; four-in-hand or bow tie. ① Summer: White linen suit.

SEMIFORMAL: DAY	SEMIFORMAL: EVENING
① Same as informal day.	① Same as informal evening.
① Same as informal day.	① Same as informal evening.
① Oxford gray business coat; white starched or pleated shirt, folded collar; striped trousers; four-in-hand tie, striped; gray or black homburg hat. ① Summer: Palm Beach suit; Panama hat. ① White linen suit; straw hat; no gloves. ① Gray or dark blue coat with white flannel trousers; white shirt; four-in-hand tie; straw hat.	① Full evening dress (see "1930s Formal Evening"). ① Tuxedo with black faille waistcoat; stiff shirt, black studs, wing collar, black bow tie; patent-leather shoes, derby or felt hat. ① Black or dark blue dinner jacket; single- or double-breasted waistcoat; white piqué shirt, fold collar; black or blue bow tie; patent-leather low evening shoes; homburg hat. ① Summer: White dinner jacket and dark slacks.
① Oxford gray business coat; white starched or pleated shirt, folded collar; striped trousers and four-in-hand tie, striped; gray or black homburg hat. ① Summer: Palm Beach suit; Panama hat. ① White linen suit; straw hat; no gloves. ① Gray or dark blue coat with white flannel trousers; white shirt; four-in-hand tie; straw hat.	① Full evening dress (see "1940s Formal Evening"). ① Tuxedo with black faille waistcoat; stiff shirt, black studs, wing collar; black bow tie; patent-leather shoes; opera hat or black homburg. ① Black or dark blue dinner jacket; single- or double-breasted waistcoat; white piqué shirt, fold collar; black or blue bow tie; patent-leather low evening shoes; homburg hat. ① Summer: White dinner jacket and dark slacks.
① Oxford gray business coat, white starched or pleated shirt, folded collar; striped trousers and four-in-hand tie, striped; gray or black homburg hat. ① Summer: White suit; gray or dark blue coat with white flannel trousers; white shirt; four-in-hand tie; straw hat.	① Tuxedo with white waistcoat optional; stiff shirt, black studs, wing collar; black bow tie; patent-leather shoes; opera hat or black homburg. ① Black or dark blue dinner jacket; single- or double-breasted waistcoat; white piqué shirt, fold collar; black or blue bow tie; patent-leather low evening shoes; homburg hat. ① Summer: White dinner jacket and dark slacks.

CLOTHING FOR THE GROOM, BY DECADE

	FORMAL DAY	FORMAL EVENING
1910S	① Frock coat with gray or matching pants, white starched shirt with wing or fold collar; white or black bow tie; gray or black top hat; black, tan, or white shoes (depending on pants color), white spats; white gloves. ① Cutaway coat with single- or double-breasted waistcoat in gray or white for summer; striped trousers; white starched shirt, wing or fold collar; ascot, necktie, or four-in-hand, in gray or black stripes or checks; black hose, black shoes with white or gray spats (optional; must match gloves); high silk hat with a curve on one or both sides; white, gray, or buff gloves.	① Frock coat with gray or matching pants; white starched shirt with wing collar; white piqué bow tie; gray or black top hat; black, tan, or white shoes (depending on pants color), white spats; white gloves. ① Tailcoat, single- or double-breasted; white starched shirt with wing collar; white piqué bow tie; white piqué V-front waistcoat; trousers match coat; black patent-leather low shoes or pumps; high black silk hat or opera hat; white kid gloves, white scarf, white handkerchief.
1920S	① Cutaway coat with single- or double-breasted waistcoat in gray or white for summer; striped trousers; white starched shirt, wing or fold collar; ascot, necktie, or four-in-hand, in gray or black stripes or checks; black hose, black shoes with white or gray spats (optional; must match gloves); high silk hat with a curve on one or both sides; white, gray, or buff gloves.	① Tailcoat, single- or double-breasted; white starched shirt with wing collar; white piqué bow tie; white piqué V-front waistcoat; trousers match coat; black patent-leather low shoes or pumps; high black silk hat or opera hat; white kid gloves, white scarf, white handkerchief.
1930S	① Cutaway coat with single- or double-breasted waistcoat in gray or white for summer; striped trousers; white starched shirt, wing or fold collar; ascot, necktie, or four-in-hand, in gray or black stripes or checks; black hose, black shoes with white or gray spats (optional; must match gloves); high silk hat; white, gray, or buff gloves.	① Tailcoat, single- or double-breasted; white starched shirt with wing collar; white piqué bow tie; white piqué V-front waistcoat; pearl studs; trousers must match coat; black patent-leather low shoes or pumps; high black silk hat or opera hat; white kid gloves, white scarf, white handkerchief.
1940S	① Cutaway coat with single- or double-breasted matching waistcoat in gray or white for summer; striped trousers; white starched shirt, wing or fold collar; ascot, necktie, or four-in-hand, in gray or black stripes or checks; black hose, black shoes; high silk hat; white, gray, or buff gloves (optional); spats (optional). ① Military uniform.	① Tailcoat, single- or double-breasted; white starched shirt with wing collar; white piqué bow tie; white piqué V-front waistcoat; pearl studs; trousers must match coat; black patent-leather low shoes or pumps; high black silk hat or opera hat; white kid gloves, white scarf, white handkerchief. ① Military uniform.
1950S	① Cutaway coat with single- or double-breasted matching waistcoat or white for summer; striped trousers; white starched shirt, wing or fold collar; ascot, necktie, or four-in-hand, in gray or black stripes or checks; black hose, black shoes; high silk hat; white, gray, or buff gloves (optional); spats (optional).	① Tailcoat, single- or double-breasted; white starched shirt with wing collar; white piqué bow tie; white piqué V-front waistcoat; pearl studs; trousers must match coat; black patent-leather low shoes or pumps; high black silk hat or opera hat; white kid gloves, white scarf, white handkerchief.

Even though zoot suits weren't considered appropriate wedding attire in the 1940s, some contemporary grooms like to wear them to evoke the spirit of the swing era. Mary Litzinger produced a 1940s wedding for Sandi and Mike Bennett of Woodland Hills, California, zooting up the groom, groomsmen, and even the little ring bearer.

(Photo: Cary Shapiro)

- When the groom wears gloves, the best man should also wear them. The groom should remove his gloves and give them to the best man as the processional walks down the aisle.
- The ties worn by the groom and the best man should be identical. The ties worn by the groomsmen should be different from those of the groom and best man.
- The groom wears a sprig from the bride's bouquet as a boutonniere, and the best man wears a different boutonniere from the groomsmen's.
- For vintage authenticity, call the groom's attendants "groomsmen" and not "ushers," as this is a more contemporary term.

The taffeta gowns worn by this 1940s bride and her maid of honor complement each other beautifully.

If you don't know a four-in-hand from a homburg, don't be concerned—they'll explain it all at the formal-wear shop. Men's wear has changed very little over the years. The only decade that might be a challenge to outfit is the 1910s, and that's only if your groom prefers to wear a frock coat. For that garment, you might need to contact a costume shop.

OUTFITTING THE BRIDESMAIDS

f you want to dress your bridesmaids in authentic vintage clothing, chances are you won't find multiple examples of the same dress. Instead, have them wear dresses the same length, from the same era. You can pick dresses all the same color or in several colors from your palette.

If you want all your bridesmaids' dresses to match, you can have dresses custom-made or sewn from authentic vintage or reproduction patterns. You might get lucky and find a selection of contemporary dresses made in a vintage style and buy them off the rack.

It's best to keep the dresses all the same length and from the same era. Make sure that the bridesmaids' dresses you select are compatible with your gown. It's best not to mix eras here, either. The women should all wear

Make sure your bridesmaids' ensembles are compatible with yours. The frilly dresses of this 1937 wedding party completely overpower the petite bride in her traditional lace gown.

PROPER DRESS LENGTHS FOR BRIDESMAIDS

1910s
Floor length
1920s
Calf length
1930s
Floor length
1940s
Floor length or street length
1950s
Ballerina length (midcalf)

Theresa LaQuey's bridesmaids wore Ginger Rogers–inspired dresses. (Photo: Laurie Gordon)

matching headpieces and carry matching bouquets. Your maid of honor's dress, headpiece, and bouquet can be slightly different, but they should complement what the bridesmaids wear and the flowers they carry.

If you're concerned that your bridesmaids won't be able to wear their dresses again, be aware that many classic styles from the 1920s through the 1950s still look contemporary. Keep this in mind when making your selections.

If you use headpieces or hats, keep them true to the look of the period. When in doubt, flowers worn in the hair always look wonderfully vintage and timeless.

Location, Location, Location

CHAPTER FIVE

very Hollywood filmmaker knows the importance of location. Months before any shooting starts, scouts comb the country to track down just the right places that suit the movie's subject matter and time period. Filming on location saves time and money—fewer sets have to be built, and custom decorations can be kept to a minimum. You can benefit the same way that Hollywood does by choosing the right location for your vintage wedding. Not only does a great period setting provide instant ambience, it saves you a lot of decorating headaches.

Just think of how much fun you'll have looking around. You can poke around grand old vintage hotels, historic mansions, and nightclubs. There are also plenty of places you might not have thought about, such as public parks and buildings, train stations, bed-and-breakfast inns, vintage ships, or museums. We bet that once you start looking, your biggest challenge won't be finding the right place, it will be deciding which place to choose.

A few important things to remember: Each venue has its own set of rules and regulations. Some places will let you hold both the ceremony and recep-

Ryan Patterson and Richard Plotkin held their wedding at the historic Ebell of Los Angeles, originally a women's club. The classic 1920s architectural details, including carved columns and ceilings and arched windows, coupled with the antique furnishings and dramatic lighting, offered the couple a perfect ready-made backdrop for their vintage event.

(Photo: Steve Streble)

tion on-site, others just the ceremony. Some will have their own catering services that they use exclusively, others will let you bring in your own. Never assume that you can hold a wedding in a public place without first getting permission and a permit.

Naturally we can't list all the possibilities in the country, but we can tell you how to research a good vintage location. To start, contact your city, county, or state historical society, historic preservation groups, museum curators, city and county parks departments, and area art deco societies. Make a list of all the historic properties in your area. Proprietors of vintage clothing shops and antiques shops can sometimes recommend interesting out-of-the-way places you may have overlooked.

The Palace of Fine Arts, San Francisco, from a 1915 postcard.

This beautiful dome of San Francisco's Palace of Fine Arts is one of the few structures remaining from the Panama Pacific Exposition of 1915. It's one of the most picturesque settings for a wedding from any era, in a city well-known for its spectacular beauty. It rents for just $350 for the first two hours, then $35 per hour after that. You can hold both your ceremony and your reception here. For booking, contact the San Francisco Permits and Reservations Department. Just as with any popular site, you'll need to reserve this location far in advance—the reservations department recommends you call at least one year ahead.

Find out about the public parks and buildings that are available in your area. They can provide interesting and often overlooked locations, as well as good values for brides and grooms on a budget.

Live near the water? Don't overlook the possibilities floating nearby. The *Queen Mary* in Long Beach is a natural, but who'd think to have a wedding on

DO-IT-YOURSELF AMBIENCE

Carrying out a vintage theme successfully through the use of a contemporary reception site or generic hotel ballroom can take a lot of hard work or extra cash. But some motivated couples prefer to work with this kind of "blank slate," where they can create exactly the environment they want. Consider Deborah Burke and Robert Hoye. They found a one-hundred-year-old house to rent for their 1910s-era wedding in Massachusetts. "It was perfect—on the outside," says Burke, who explains that the inside was a different story. "The furniture was contemporary and really awful," she said. "There was no way this was going to work, so we decided to fix the situation ourselves."

The morning of their wedding, she and her husband-to-be drove a truckload of antique furniture from their house and moved it all into the wedding site. "Empire couches, wicker chairs, Eastlake dressers, end tables, old framed pictures, piano shawls . . . you name it, we moved it," Burke said. "We wanted the house to look lived-in, as though it really were our home." After three hours of setup, they went back to their empty house, changed into their wedding clothes, and came back for the ceremony and reception. Hours later, after everybody left, they got back into their jeans and struck the set, moving it all back into the truck that night.

Was it worth it? "We wouldn't have had it any other way," says Burke, laughing. "We were exhausted, but it was great to have everything exactly the way we wanted."

a 1940s naval vessel? You can, and what a great idea. The SS *Jeremiah O'Brien* is docked at Pier 32 just south of the San Francisco Bay Bridge. As part of your reception, you and your guests can tour the ship, which was part of the original D-Day armada.

Cover the waterfront in your area and see what vintage vessels you can

MARRYING WITHIN THEIR STATION

Teresa L. Scott married Frederick M. Joseph at New York's Grand Central Terminal on October 29, 1995. Scott explains why the grand old Grand Central was exactly the place for them:

""When we decided to get married, we didn't want it to be in a religious institution or a 'wedding mill,' and we didn't want it to be in a place that wasn't going to be here fifty years from now. I'm an architecture buff, and I love Grand Central Station—I always take a detour through it if I can. It's so beautiful and representative of New York City. It also has cathedral-like qualities without the religious overtones. So I called the MTA and they said, 'Wow! No one's ever thought of that.' They were very excited to have the first wedding there. After the ceremony, a jazz band went right into 'I Feel Good' by James Brown. That was our recessional. We immediately started dancing, while the MTA flashed 'Congratulations!' on the monitors.""

The couple sent out wedding invitations using a subway token motif in bronze, with the token's Y-shape cut out on the front. The reply card showed an image of the east balcony of Grand Central terminal, where the ceremony took place. The invitation included another clever touch: a pair of subway tokens for guests to use when traveling to and from the wedding.

find—from ocean liners in dry dock, to multimasted sailing schooners, to ferryboats and paddlewheelers.

The restored Union Terminal in Cincinnati is the site of many Ohio weddings throughout the year. Hold your reception in the station's private dining rooms or under the grand rotunda with its wonderful 1930s murals. This Art

A reception hall doesn't have to be fancy to be retrofestive. This old tap room would be a wonderfully unstuffy place for an informal 1930s–1950s wedding reception.

Deco station, which was built in 1933 as part of the Works Progress Administration, is in great demand. The average $1,000 rental fee covers the facility, including tables and chairs.

Many of the wonderful old train stations in the country have been renovated and offer banquet facilities. Check with your local historical societies to see if there are any renovated WPA buildings in your area as possibilities for an offbeat and stylish Art Deco–era venue.

If you ever thought about getting hitched on the observation deck of the Empire State Building, think again. You can pop the question there, but if you want to say your I dos at King Kong's favorite hangout, you'll need to rent one

Union Terminal, Cincinnati, Ohio, 1940s.

of the conference rooms on the 80th or 102nd floors. You can have your ceremony there, but not your reception. And you can't get hitched between Memorial Day and Labor Day because transporting your wedding party up and down the elevators would cause a traffic jam for the tourists on the observation deck. All these rules for $520 an hour? We say, "Fuggeddaboudit!"

The management of other, less tourist-ridden historic buildings may be more accommodating. If you have a favorite vintage edifice in your area, call the management staff and see if there's a reception room that looks as good as the building does from the lobby.

The 1974 film *The Great Gatsby* was shot on location at Rosecliff, one of the great mansions of Newport, Rhode Island, built in 1902. You can rent the same room where Redford and Farrow romanced, but it will set you back at least $4,000 for four hours.

Other Newport mansions host weddings, too, but are equally pricey. You can book your wedding at the Astors' Beechwood Victorian Living

A cocktail napkin from the Empire State Building, 1930s.

EMPIRE STATE OBSERVATORY · WORLD'S TALLEST BUILDING

Above: Gardens in the Mabel and John Ringling Museum, Sarasota, Florida, 1940s.

Right: The Palace nightclub, Sunnyvale, California, 1999.

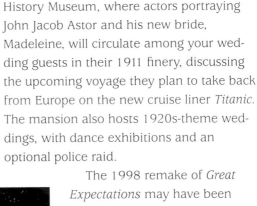

History Museum, where actors portraying John Jacob Astor and his new bride, Madeleine, will circulate among your wedding guests in their 1911 finery, discussing the upcoming voyage they plan to take back from Europe on the new cruise liner *Titanic*. The mansion also hosts 1920s-theme weddings, with dance exhibitions and an optional police raid.

The 1998 remake of *Great Expectations* may have been filmed at circus impresario John Ringling's home, but Miss Havisham doesn't haunt the gardens of the John and Mabel Ringling Museum of Art, which can be your site for a beautiful vintage wedding. Rent the rose garden for $250, the museum courtyard for $2,500.

Historic Mediterranean-revival buildings make wonderful settings for period weddings. You can find churches, hotels, mansions, museums, theaters, and many other kinds of buildings in this style, large and small, throughout the American South, West, and Southwest.

In the early 1990s, an abandoned and run-down 1930s theater in Sunnyvale, California, was converted into the Palace. The exterior of this elegant nightclub is pure Art Deco, but the interior has been renovated in a sophisticated neo-Gothic style, and the two work together surprisingly well. The Palace has become a hot place for cool events in Silicon Valley, including many weddings.

If you live in a city with older neighborhoods, look for an authentic vintage nightclub that hasn't changed much since the 1940s. The 1990s swing dancing revival also means that you'll likely have a number of "new vintage" nightclubs to choose from, especially in bigger cities.

SHOOTING VINTAGE-STYLE PHOTOGRAPHY

fter your wedding day has come and gone, you're left with your memories . . . and, of course, your photographs. One of the most enduring and important things you can do to remember your vintage wedding is to take a selection of photos in an authentic style.

But what does this mean? Can contemporary photographers using today's technology adapt to a vintage style? How much "old style" do you really want? And how do you find photographers who know how to work this way?

Just married: A Chicago couple exits their church, 1937.

THE BASICS, IN BLACK AND WHITE

The first thing that always comes to mind when thinking of vintage photography is black-and-white film, which was the medium for almost every photograph taken before World War II. And even though color photography became popular in the 1950s, most professional wedding photos taken that decade were still shot in classic black and white.

The style of photography also changed through the decades as technology advanced. If you look at wedding pictures from the 1910s and 1920s, you won't see any candid shots or pictures of classic wedding rituals. What you'll

THE TRADITIONAL PHOTO PACKAGE

We found a list of traditional wedding photos in a mid-1950s wedding workbook. At vintage weddings of the 1930s–1950s, these posed photos marked the most sentimental wedding moments and were often the only pictures a photographer took, other than the formal portraits of the wedding party.

"Contemporary photographers sometimes skip the classic posed shots," says San Francisco photographer Laurie Gordon, "and that's too bad, because these images are so characteristic of the period." To keep the look authentic, print these photos in eight-by-ten black and white.

- Last-minute dressing: arranging the bride's veil in the mirror
- The bride arriving at the ceremony, getting out of the car
- The bride, her attendants, and her father at the start of the processional
- Recessional
- Receiving line
- Cutting the cake
- Feeding each other the cake
- First dance
- Tossing the bouquet
- Running through the rice storm (leaving the reception)
- Getting into the car (shot from inside the car)
- Waving through the side or back window of the car as it pulls away

A classic posed image of a bride with her attendants, 1949.

(Photo: George Fries)

see are a lot of formal portraits of the bride and groom and the wedding party. This is because photographic equipment wasn't very portable yet and film speed was slow. As a result, photographers shot formal wedding portraits in their studios and in rooms where natural window light could effectively illuminate their subjects.

All of this changed in the 1930s and 1940s with the introduction of flash photography, faster film, and handheld cameras. But even then photographers couldn't shoot hundreds of photos in rapid succession as they can today; there were no motorized drives to advance the film automatically. At the average wedding in those days, photographers had just enough time to set

Direct lighting can help create dramatic and theatrical-looking portraits. Laurie Gordon shoots many of her studio wedding photos in this style, including this one of Marilyn Ambra Thorpe. "This is how the classic movie stills were taken," Gordon says. "Natural lighting just can't provide that wonderful Hollywood glamour look that people love." (Photo: Laurie Gordon)

up, compose, and shoot ten to twelve standard wedding events. Wedding photographers typically sold this to brides as a wedding "package." After the bride approved the photos from a set of proofs, they were made into eight-by-ten-inch prints and delivered in an album a few weeks after the wedding.

PORTRAIT STYLE, THROUGH THE YEARS

Florida photographer Christopher Bunn has been shooting portrait photography for many years and is a devotee of vintage techniques and equipment. He explained how portrait photography evolved in the twentieth century. "Up until the end of the 1920s, portrait photographers used natural window light to illuminate their subjects in the studio. You can see this in the portraits from this era; the shadows are very soft."

An elegant 1940s wedding portrait, shot in front of an elaborate painted backdrop.

But in the 1930s and 1940s, the look of studio portraits changed, Bunn says, as photographers began using more sophisticated lighting techniques to create special effects. This new style of photography required a delicate balancing act between light and shadow, requiring skill on the part of the photographer not just to compose the image, but to aim the lights in the most flattering and artistic way. "For example, a photographer might use a spotlight to light the face, floodlights to minimize shadows on the face, and several spotlights to play up highlights on the hair and shoulders," Bunn says. "Because of the challenges presented by light and shadow, glamour is a difficult type of photography to do well." And because this is an older and more time-consuming technique, not all photographers know how to work in this style.

"This isn't a time to be working with an amateur or a photographer who is experimenting," says Bunn. "There's a level of knowledge and expertise needed to balance and direct the lights. Don't forget that in addition to the classic glamour stills, they shot horror pictures this way, too!" Bunn adds that many portrait photographers of the 1930s and 1940s still preferred to shoot using natural and indirect light, so you'll see both kinds of lighting in wedding portraits from this era. "Look at the shadows to see if they're soft and fuzzy or hard and distinct. If they're hard, then they used floods and spots."

Most contemporary portrait photographers are used to shooting with indirect light using either natural light or light banks powered with strobes. But it's tougher to find a good portrait photographer who works in the 1930s and 1940s style. Be sure to ask about his or her experience taking black-and-white portraits in the old Hollywood glamour style. And, of course, take a careful look at the photographer's portfolio. Judge the photographs not only by their composition, but also by how attractively and creatively the photographer has lit his subjects.

AUTHENTIC PROPS COMPLETE THE PICTURE

Another important ingredient that marks a portrait as vintage is the use of period visual elements. Gordon's clients are lucky enough to pose in front of authentic painted backdrops, salvaged from an old photo studio. But if your

Laurie Gordon likes to shoot portraits of brides holding family wedding pictures. This is especially effective if the bride wears an heirloom gown, as Lauren Livermore does here. (Photo: Laurie Gordon)

photographer doesn't have these (and most won't), you can stage a similar setting with props, either in the studio or on location elsewhere.

By browsing through old wedding photographs, you can get a good idea of the classic portrait props and poses because there are so many consistent elements. Up through the 1920s, either the bride or groom sat in a decorative chair, usually made of wicker, most often with the groom seated and the bride standing next to him with her hand upon his shoulder. Sometimes the bride sat, but she usually stood in order to show off her gown and bouquet. Couples posed on patterned Oriental rugs and alongside potted ferns or palms. Sometimes the image was framed by an architectural element such as decorative pillars, an old fireplace, a bay window, or an arch. If weather permits, you might use a decorative garden niche, with an old-fashioned bench,

Your guests will appreciate a memento from your wedding, especially a vintage-style photograph of themselves. Set up a photo station at the reception with vintage props. If you can arrange it, use a classic car as a backdrop. Slip instant pictures into custom-made vintage-style photo jackets, or mail the pictures to the guests after the wedding, perhaps along with your thank-you notes.

It's a great idea to hand-tint some of your favorite black-and-white wedding portraits, a favorite technique used in the years before color photography. Hire an expert to color the photos or learn to do it yourself.

fountain, gazebo, or trellis. And of course, wouldn't it be perfect to have your 1930s portrait taken in an authentic Art Deco building?

REVIVING THE CLASSIC WEDDING PORTRAIT

It's perfectly acceptable, sometimes preferable, to hire one photographer to take your portrait and another to shoot your wedding and reception. Many portrait photographers don't shoot weddings, and some wedding photographers aren't experienced enough to light vintage portraits properly. Those who are fluent in both styles, like Gordon, seem to be the exception rather than the rule. She recommends that today's vintage brides revive the old-fashioned tradition of having a formal studio portrait taken up to a month before the wedding day.

"Contemporary brides are deprived of this wonderful tradition," says Gordon. "The formal portrait was an opportunity for the bride to have a dress rehearsal weeks before the wedding, to test her hairstyle and makeup, and to start feeling like a real bride. In the whirlwind of the wedding day, a bride doesn't get to experience being a bride for very long. When she has her wedding portrait taken, she has the opportunity to be a bride not once, but twice."

The studio setting also provides a more relaxed atmosphere for the portrait session. Not only are the bride and groom busy with guests and family on their wedding day, but the photographer is also under a lot of pressure. "On the day of the wedding, there's too much commotion to set up, light, and shoot a portrait the right way," says Gordon, "and sometimes there's no good place to do it."

The "right way" for Gordon often includes shooting her brides or couples in vintage settings or in front of authentic painted backdrops—lit, composed, and styled in a way that evokes Hollywood glamour. After years of studying vintage wedding photographs for the most interesting compositions, Gordon re-creates some of the most charming and sentimental among them, such as the classic image of the bride with the bridesmaids' bouquets placed along her train.

She also recommends that the bride and groom have their portrait taken together, dismissing the old superstition that a groom shouldn't see the bride in her gown before the wedding. "This is the most overrated tradition," Gordon says. "It didn't even exist in the day when formal wedding portraits of couples were taken all the time. People shouldn't let this stand in their way of a memory that will last a lifetime."

FINDING THE COLOR IN BLACK AND WHITE

Should you hire just any photographer to shoot a vintage wedding? No, says Gordon. She recommends using an experienced wedding photographer who is also experienced in black-and-white photography. "A wedding has a unique rhythm and a pace. It's hard for photographers to adapt to this if they're not used to it," she says. "It's also important to work with someone who understands classic black-and-white documentary style," says Gordon, "as in the old *Life* magazine style of photojournalism, and not the contemporary use of this word, which has come to mean edgy, angular, and blurry. The two styles are very different. One is vintage, one is not."

Special Vintage Touches for the Ceremony and Reception

Keeping Things Ceremonious

e haven't written much about the ceremony yet, and there's an important reason why. We feel that your wedding ceremony is one of the most personal moments of your life, and the two of you should decide how to conduct this part of your day. If you're marrying in a church or synagogue, let the combination of the atmosphere, the clothing, and the floral arrangements carry the vintage mood. Depending upon your religion and the rules of the church or synagogue, you may be allowed to substitute certain vintage music for the period before the service as well as for your processional and recessional; but we encourage you to pick music that reflects the dignity of the service and is respectful of your house of worship.

If you're marrying in a nontraditional ceremony outside of a church or synagogue, you can be a bit less conservative. If you've picked a good vintage location for the ceremony, you might not need to do much decorating. Be sure the caterer uses wooden folding chairs and not metal ones. Florists can help carry out your theme by using arches, tulle, greenery, and other architectural elements. Some have access to theatrical stage props or architectural

In a northern California vineyard, Lisa Hewitt and Mark Koester strutted away from the altar to live 1920s music. Adding to the festive garden atmosphere, they provided their guests with colorful Chinese paper parasols to keep the sun at bay.

(Photo: Laurie Gordon)

antiques. Tonya Castleman's florist dressed up her wedding site in a dramatic way by using framed stained-glass windows, giant palms in pots on cast-iron bases, and two vintage harps dressed with lilies and candles.

For nontraditional services, you can also try incorporating appropriate vintage music into your processional and recessional. Browse through the lists of songs in chapter 2 for ideas. It's wonderful to cap off your ceremony by using a favorite upbeat tune for your recessional, such as "In the Mood" or "Fly Me to the Moon."

For an early 1940s-style wedding, events specialist Mary Litzinger worked with a lighting company to project dramatic images on the wall of a hotel ballroom. Each table was named for a different period movie star and was set in the style of a 1940s supper club. (Photo: Timothy Teague)

ADDING VINTAGE TOUCHES TO THE RECEPTION

here's a lot you can do to make a vintage reception more fun, especially in the key areas of decoration, entertainment, and food. If you've picked a good vintage venue, much of your decorating is already done for you. But there are a few extra things you can do to make the environment a bit more festive.

SETTING THE TABLES, ECLECTICALLY

Sometimes floral centerpieces just aren't enough. Crystal Zeadow hunted down flea market finds to use in handcrafting the forty-five vintage centerpieces she needed for her wedding. On top of a mirrored dresser tray on each table she arranged such items as beaded purses, pieces of fringed trim, tassels, jewelry boxes, strands of pearls, cosmetics, compacts, vintage postcards, framed sheet music, and vintage hats. She included a candle and a fresh flower in each arrangement.

Tonya Castleman also rummaged for months, seeking out orphaned pieces of china and silverware from flea markets and thrift shops to make beauti-

Encourage your guests to dress in period clothing by providing the names of local vintage clothing shops, including those that will rent outfits. You may be surprised by how many show up dressed to the nines. (Photo: Laurie Gordon)

fully eclectic place settings at her reception. At each setting she included a few original vintage linen postcards of the area as favors for the guests. A lot of work? Yes. A lot of fun? Absolutely. Both women say that the treasure hunt was a blast.

INVOLVING THE GUESTS

For the past few years, Laurie Gordon has suggested a new reception tradition to her brides that's not only decorative, but allows the guests to be involved in the wedding. She recommends that couples set up a special table where guests can bring framed pictures of their own weddings to display. "Guests really enjoy looking at all the pictures. If there are elderly people there, they sometimes bring the most incredible vintage photographs," she

When staging 1940s-era weddings, consultant Mary Litzinger likes to outfit a cigarette girl to circulate among the guests, giving out treats such as bubble-gum cigars, real stogies with custom cigar bands, candy cigarettes, and custom-designed matchbooks. She also hires a photo girl to walk from table to table and take souvenir pictures of the guests, just as they did in the old nightclubs.

(Photo:Timothy Teague)

says. "It makes people feel involved, helps them to meet others they may not know at the wedding, and gives them something fun to do."

THE SWEETEST SOUNDS

I don't have to convince anyone reading this book about how wonderful vintage music is. Whether live or recorded, it's an optional part of your ceremony, but an essential part of your reception. With the recent craze for big band and swing music, it's easier than ever to find a band that can perform the great old songs. But even if you can't have a live band at your wedding, you can still have great music by hiring a disc jockey to spin some vintage CDs. How else could you claim that Frank Sinatra sang at your wedding?

If you have a public radio station nearby that plays vintage music, see if any of the disc jockeys moonlight and do weddings. If you hire a wedding disc jockey, be sure to give him a playlist ahead of time with the artists and songs you want to hear. Use

First dance for the Cunninghams, 1951.

(Photo: Walter Leamy)

the music and musicians listed in chapter 2 to help you hit the highlights. Another good idea is to lend the disc jockey a few CDs from your collection or buy a few new CDs as a wedding gift to yourselves. There are some excellent remastered and reissued compilations on the market today that make the selection easy. One record label we particularly like is Past Perfect Records (see "Resources"), which sells exclusively over the Internet. Other good vintage record labels to investigate include Rhino, Sony, Columbia, Capitol, Verve, MCA/Universal, and Hip-O.

Vary the mood by including several different kinds of music at your reception. For the cocktail party, when people are talking, eating, and mingling, hire a pianist or an a cappella vocal group. Use the dance band to rev up the last half of the reception, when it's time to work off the rumaki and Swedish meatballs.

FOOD AND FUN: REINVENTING THE VINTAGE WEDDING CAKE

Our wedding cake is a focal point of your reception, a perfect opportunity to create something special that ties in to your vintage theme. But in order to understand how to make your wedding cake even better, it's helpful to learn how these cakes originally came about.

The timeless cake ritual, 1949.

(Photo: George Fries)

LET THEM EAT CAKE . . . OFF THE FLOOR

At ancient Roman weddings, a groom would take a bite of a cake or biscuit and break the rest over his bride's head as an homage to the god Jupiter. (One can only hope, for her

Wedding reception held in a Florida church, early 1950s.

sake, that it wasn't stale.) Guests were then permitted to eat any fragments that fell on the floor. The Romans took this custom with them when they invaded the rest of Europe, where it was practiced for centuries even after the Romans were gone. The ceremony evolved into a good-luck superstition to ensure fertility, hospitality, and prosperity—and at some blessed point, guests were no longer asked to eat off the ground.

The original Roman cake recipe was lost over the years, but we know that in the 1700s and 1800s, wedding cakes were made with aromatic ingredients such as rosewater, orange flower water, musk, and ambergris (that's right, many of the same ingredients used to make perfume). Cakes were frosted with an icing made of sugar and bitter almonds, said to represent the mingled pleasure and pain that accompanies married life.

Early-twentieth-century wedding cakes tasted somewhat better than the ancient perfumed concoctions, but the selection of flavors was still rather limited. Amy Vanderbilt describes the standard choices as "the silver cake, made with egg whites alone, and is light and airy; a yellow pound cake, which is richer; and the dark, rich fruit cake, most expensive of all." In these earlier decades, wedding cakes were always frosted in white, decorated with sugary pastel flowers and leaves, and trimmed with a ribbon of frosting squeezed from a pastry tube.

REMEMBERING THE RING CAKE

What we now call the wedding cake used to be called the bride's cake. At some weddings this cake would be baked into the shape of a giant diamond ring or a pair of intertwined wedding bands. The bride and groom's initials were written in icing, with hers on the left and his on the right; and the inside of the ring or rings was decorated with flowers matching those in the bridal bouquet.

These "ring cakes" sometimes had miniature fortune-telling favors baked into them, a popular custom that was also practiced in cakes served on Halloween and at Mardi Gras time in New Orleans. The favors represented a variety of good fortunes related to romance and everyday life. For example, if your piece contained a tiny ring, you'd be the next to marry; or if you found a tiny ship in your cake, you'd soon take a voyage. Guests enjoyed discovering the favors within the cake and comparing their respective fortunes.

A ring cake at an informal wedding, early 1950s.

REVIVING THE RING CAKE TRADITION

$\mathscr{J}$f you decide to have a ring cake at your wedding, remember that guests in decades past knew to watch out for the favors in the cake. But it's a safe bet that your guests never saw one of these cakes before, so be sure to tell them that their piece of cake might contain a small favor and to be very careful when chewing. To be on the safe side, make sure that the favors are big enough so they can't be swallowed and that they're made from a nontoxic material that won't melt. When baking the cake, spread the favors evenly inside the ring. While it's not necessary that all guests find a favor in their piece of cake, it's considered good luck if they do.

HERE COMES THE BRIDE'S CAKE

Most people envision the multitiered bride's cake when they think of weddings. The cake tiers rest directly atop one another or are separated by risers, sometimes in the shape of tiny architectural columns. The top tier of vintage cakes was invariably crowned with a choice of sugar flowers; real flowers; arches with bells, doves, or swans; or tiny brides and grooms made of plastic or porcelain. Known as cake toppers, the figural brides and grooms are hot collectibles today. The earliest examples first appeared in the 1920s and were made of celluloid. Many figural cake toppers of the 1920s and 1930s were in the form of kewpielike children instead of adults.

Tradition called for basic white or yellow cake on the wedding day. To demonstrate how little creativity went into the ingredients a few decades ago, we found this uninspired bride's cake recipe in an Emily Post wedding planner:

> 3 packages white cake mix
> 3¾ cups water
> 6 egg whites
> 1½ teaspoons almond extract
> Ornamental frosting

If you're striving for historical accuracy, we urge you to consider this an important place to break from tradition, as the white or yellow bride's cake is not terribly exciting. If you're going to the time, trouble, and expense of having a wedding cake, why not have one made with interesting flavors everyone will enjoy?

THE ALL-IMPORTANT CAKE DESIGN

Your wedding cake might be contemporary on the inside, but it can look vintage on the outside. Bakers offer a standard selection of traditional designs to choose from, or they'll work with you to create a custom design. If you can afford it, get a fantastic one-of-a-kind cake for your vintage reception. After a

An Art Deco light fixture at the San Francisco Western Merchandise Mart inspired this wedding cake, suggested by Laurie Gordon and created by Cakework, San Francisco.

(Photo: Laurie Gordon)

Gary Chapman poses with a selection of his award-winning wedding cakes.

𝒜 sample of the flavors of wedding cake offered by London cake designer Gary Chapman:

Dark chocolate chip

Orange and Grand Marnier

Lemon and coconut

Cherry, ground almond, and Amaretto

Zesty lemon

Piña colada

Raspberry ripple

Coffee and Kahlúa

Traditional rich fruit

Orange and chocolate

Chocolate and walnut

Benedictine

Vanilla Madeira

meeting to discuss your theme and ideas, the cake designer will create up to half a dozen sketches for you to select from. Be sure to bring any pictures, magazine articles, clippings, fabric samples, or anything else that can help inspire a design.

Some bakers have a firm foundation in early-twentieth-century design. Gary Chapman creates award-winning wedding cakes in London. His muse is Dolly Tree, who designed fashions for stage and screen in the early twentieth century, including for the *Ziegfeld Follies*, Myrna Loy, and others. Chapman creates custom cakes that pick up design elements from the bride's dress, the wedding invitation, or other relevant details. Chapman doesn't miss an opportunity to incorporate period design elements into his cakes, especially those inspired by vintage fashion.

To ensure that you're communicating properly with your cake designer, bring pictures with you. Approve the design from a good sketch. If you find you're not on the same wavelength, disengage politely and find another baker to work with. Be sure to look at the baker's portfolio of cakes to see if they're up to the job. It also helps to get references.

FRUITCAKE FOR THE GROOM

Along with the bride's cake, most vintage weddings included a groom's cake, which was a heavy black fruitcake soaked in liquor. This cake wasn't meant to be eaten at the reception. Instead guests took a small piece home in a box. In 1952, Amy Vanderbilt described the cake as "wrapped in foil and boxed in tiny, white, satin-tied boxes . . . a luxury these days because of the hand-labor they entail." This is the cake, according to tradition, that the guests put under their pillows in order to dream of their one true love. How much got slept on and how much was eaten is something we'll never know. Unquestionably a charming wedding tradition, groom's cake fell out of favor by the 1950s, as Vanderbilt noted. Like many handmade things, it simply became too impractical and expensive.

TIP: REVIVING THE GROOM'S CAKE

*T*he groom's cake is a wonderful old tradition that you can revive for your vintage wedding.

Ask your caterer to bake a cake in any flavor you prefer, or do it yourself if you want to. Today most people don't care for fruitcake, so feel free to pick something else—but be sure to use a flavor that's different from that of the bride's cake. A sparsely frosted cake with a moist, dense texture is easiest to cut and box. Since you'll be cutting it up anyway, it doesn't need to be elaborately designed, just delicious. The cake should be made big enough so that each guest can get a small piece to take home, about the size of a brownie.

You can get inexpensive premade gift boxes in almost any color, each one sold flat and assembled in a snap. Silver boxes are especially nice, tied with white ribbons. At the reception, enlist the help of a bridesmaid or groomsman to cut and wrap the pieces of cake in a napkin and pack them in the boxes as guests depart. The boxes and ribbon ties can be preassembled and stashed under a table to save time, but for freshness it's best not to cut the cake and pack the boxes until the guests are about to depart. As a nice finishing touch, add tiny cards to the ribbons that explain the groom's cake tradition and the meaning of dreams.

OLD-FASHIONED CATERING: THE WEDDING BREAKFAST

*T*oday most weddings include a reception party, often a big affair in a fancy location, including expensive food, cocktails, and entertainment. But in the past only the wealthiest brides and grooms could afford this kind of celebration. Average couples had small wedding ceremonies at home

It's an old custom to sleep on a piece of groom's cake in order to dream of your one true love. But be careful what else you might dream about. We consulted *Princess Yvonne's Dream Book*, a 1920s guide to the meaning of dreams, for the full scoop:

- If you dream of your **sweetheart,** you will have a happy married life.
- If you **hear bells** during a dream, this is a signal of prosperity and a wedding.
- If a young woman dreams that she is a **bride,** she may expect an inheritance.
- To dream of **kissing a bride** means a reunion between lovers.
- To **witness a happy marriage** in a dream is a good sign and denotes pleasure and happiness.
- If you are a **party to a marriage** in the dream, you will soon receive bad news.
- Dreaming of a **ring** denotes good business relations, many happy friends, travel, and success in love affairs.
- If a man dreams that he is a **bachelor,** he should avoid women, as this is a warning. If a woman dreams about a **bachelor,** the dream denotes impure love for another.
- To dream that your **youth** has been restored denotes that you will be happily married and content.

or at their place of worship, with a simple punch-and-cake reception afterward.

A tradition for couples who married in the morning or at noon (quite common in vintage times) was to have a wedding breakfast after the ceremony. "Breakfast" is something of a misnomer, as it was actually a three-course seated lunch or a two-course lunch buffet. Depending upon the circumstances of the couple, they may have invited all of their guests to the wedding break-

Digging into the fruit cup at a late 1940s formal reception.

fast or just the wedding party, family, and close friends.

According to Amy Vanderbilt, the wedding breakfast included "a soup course, such as hot clam broth with whipped cream, a main dish, such as sweetbreads *en broche* with green peas and potato balls, plus small biscuits and lettuce salad, and for dessert ice cream in fancy molds, petits fours, demitasses and of course, the bridal champagne or at least a fine white wine . . . sometimes both."

In 1922, *Home Arts and Entertainment* magazine called the wedding breakfast "a very smart form of entertainment, that is held any time between 11:30 A.M. and 1:30 P.M. The menu is precisely what one would serve for luncheon, and it may be elaborate or simple as desired. The tablecloth should hang twelve inches or more over the edge of table, and the prettiest china, glassware and silver should be used." Their suggested menu: First course, bouillon with breadsticks or buttered rolls. Second course, hot dish, such as creamed meat or fish in timbales or puff paste; tiny croquettes; Newburgs; or deviled crabs. Third course, dessert, which usually consists of two ices molded together, served with small fancy cakes or wedding cake.

WEDDING BREAKFAST MENUS, 1930

*I*f you'd like to revive this old tradition, here are some sample wedding breakfast menus from the Good Housekeeping Institute, 1930.

EARLY WEDDING BREAKFASTS

1 Orange baskets filled with orange sections
   Creamed fish (scallops, crab flakes, or salmon)
   Popovers with strawberry jam
   Coffee, cream

2 Halves of grapefruit or melon
   Halves of broiled chicken (or squab on buttered
      toast)
   Cornbread
   Currant jelly or currant preserves
   Coffee, cream

ELEVEN O'CLOCK WEDDING BREAKFASTS

1 Fruit cocktail
   Olives, celery, nuts
   Lobster or crab patties, peas
   Buttered Parker House rolls
   Hearts of lettuce
   Cheese sticks, French dressing
   Chocolate ice cream with peach sauce
   Cakes, bonbons
   Coffee, cream

2 Fruit cocktail
   Scalloped shrimp in ramekins
   Filet of beef (individual service)
   Mushroom sauce
   French-fried potatoes, hot rolls
   Spinach salad, toasted crackers
   Fruit ices, assorted flavors
   Cakes, candied fruits, coffee

A WEDDING CAKE, A BOWL OF PUNCH, AND THOU

*E*ven as late as 1958, wedding planning guides stated that most weddings were followed by a simple reception that included punch, cake, nuts and mints, and coffee or tea. You already have recipes for the cake, so here are two examples of old-fashioned wedding punch. Spiking is optional.

1 quart orange juice

1 quart grapefruit juice

1 package unsweetened Jell-O (your choice of flavors)

1½ cups sugar

2 cups water

2 quarts ginger ale

Makes 50 servings in sherbet cups. Color ice cubes with artificial coloring. Place pieces of fruit or edible flowers in ice cubes.

3 cups boiling water

¼ cup tea leaves

3 cups sugar syrup

3 cups orange juice

1 cup lemon juice

3 cups canned pineapple juice

1½ quarts ginger ale or carbonated water

Sliced fruit

Makes 50 servings. Pour boiling water over the tea leaves, steep 5 minutes. Strain and cool. Combine syrup, tea, and fruit juices. Add ginger ale or carbonated water when ready to serve. This produces a tea-colored punch. Garnish with thin slices of oranges, lemon, limes, or sliced strawberries.

JENNIFER PARKER AND SANDERS STANTON:
NOW PLAYING: "SACRED VOWS"

ennifer Parker is the assistant costume designer for *Nash Bridges,* a television show set in San Francisco. She got married on April 4, 1998, on Treasure Island, between San Francisco and Oakland. She described the event to us:

"My boss, the costume designer Richard von Ernst, took a real interest in my wedding and encouraged me to pick a theme. I decided on the 1940s, mostly because of my love of the music and the dancing. I've been into swing dancing for ages and have worn vintage clothes for a long time. The 1940s clothes are so wearable.

"Richard wanted to design my dress. He's so well versed in period clothing and wanted me to do something very true to the era. I wanted a dress I could dance in at the reception, but he said that he really liked the way trains look, too. So he made a silk chiffon dress with a silk satin

Jennifer Parker and Sanders Stanton pose next to the getaway car after the reception. (Photo: Ralph Granich)

Cheech Marin officiated at the ceremony on Treasure Island in San Francisco Bay. (Photo: Ralph Granich)

Jennifer's boss (costume designer Richard von Ernst) and his friends came nattily dressed as uniformed naval officers. (Photo: Ralph Granich)

The drop-dead authentic Parker/Stanton wedding party. (Photo: Ralph Granich)

redingote overdress that I could take off at the reception. It had all the great 1940s styling—it was fitted through the waist, had a sweetheart neckline, and had sleeves that gathered and then fit tightly. I wore my hair in rolls and wore a snood with a gardenia.

"Richard is Mr. Detail, so everything was perfect. It all looked great, from the invitation, to the bridesmaids, to my going-away outfit. For the invitations, we took a dramatic photo and designed the invitation to look like an old movie poster. We called our wedding "Sacred Vows" and included all the other information—playing at this date, at this location, starring Jennifer Parker and Sanders Stanton, and costarring Cheech Marin, who officiated at the ceremony. We suggested in the invitation that guests wear 1940s clothes. We were surprised and happy when most of the guests came in period outfits.

"We got married on Treasure Island, which is where the 1939–1940 Golden Gate International Exposition was held. After the fair closed, it became a naval base. Our friend Roberto drove us out there in his 1937 Chevrolet. We had the services in a small chapel on the island that was built for the servicemen, very simple and understated, with stained glass in a circle over the altar.

"Hydrangeas were the foundation of my color scheme, with all those great blues and purples. We decorated the chapel with hydrangeas and tulle. The reception was at Casa de la Vista, also on the island. We put potted hydrangeas wrapped in tulle on the reception tables and strung up little white lights outside. We even had hydrangeas on our cake.

The Golden Gate Bridge makes a dramatic backdrop for the bride and her bridesmaids.

(Photo: Ralph Granich)

"Richard and his friends surprised us by wearing navy uniforms to the wedding. I saw them as I was walking down the aisle and couldn't believe it, they looked so great. I've got a picture of all of us together, and it looks just as if it were taken at the end of the war.

"The bridesmaids looked just like the Andrews Sisters. Their dresses were made from real 1940s patterns. They wore platform shoes and had hats with silk hydrangeas and netting. Cheech wore a vintage tux. He loves vintage clothing. The men in the wedding party wore cutaway coats and gray vests, with striped ties.

"We had great music at the reception. The swing band Atomic Cocktail performed, and everybody danced all night. My going-away outfit was a red gabardine 1940s suit that I got at Ambience on Haight Street. I wore it with a black fedora, black platform sandals, and seamed hose. It was such a great time, we'll never forget how wonderful it all was."

MARILYN AMBRA AND NELSON THORPE: 1930S ART DECO ELEGANCE

arilyn Ambra and Nelson Thorpe's ultraformal 1930s Art Deco wedding was held on April 10, 1999, at Saint Margaret Mary Church in Oakland, California, a Gothic-style cathedral built in 1931. Marilyn and Nelson both love the Art Deco period and are active in the Art Deco Society of California. Nelson has a long-standing fondness for vintage automobiles and has owned and restored many throughout the years.

After their nuptial mass, the couple was chauffeured in a vintage 1950s Bentley to a reception at the Bellevue Club in Oakland, a private ladies' club that was built in 1929. Entering the Bellevue is like stepping back in time, as most of the furnishings and appointments are original.

Marilyn's 1930s-style gown was custom-made by Theresa LaQuey of Oakland and Autumn Adamme of Dark Garden in San Francisco. It was made of blush-colored silk charmeuse and had an astonishing eighteen feet of exquisite Art Deco cubist floral embroidery on the train. Her authentic 1930s head-

The newlywed Thorpes by the door of Saint Margaret Mary Church in Oakland, California.

(Photo: Laurie Gordon)

piece was trimmed with wax orange blossoms. She carried a cascading bouquet of orchids, gardenias, and calla lilies, trimmed with ribbons and lovers' knots. Nelson wore a tailcoat, with a white waistcoat, white tie, and gloves.

Marilyn's maid of honor wore gold and carried cymbidium orchids. The bridesmaids wore silver and carried gardenias. The attendants all wore flowers in their hair.

The guests arrived for a cocktail reception, accompanied by a piano performance of 1920s and 1930s music. This was followed by a seated dinner, the cake ceremony, and dancing to period music by the Royal Society Six, a subset of the Royal Society Jazz Orchestra.

A week before the wedding, Marilyn sat for a formal portrait session with

A 1950s Bentley got the wedding party to the church safe and dry, despite a stormy day.

(Photo: Peter Marcus)

San Francisco photographer Laurie Gordon, who took photographs in and around Marilyn and Nelson's beautiful 1920s-era home. It was a perfect backdrop befitting the elegance and style of Marilyn's gorgeous wedding ensemble.

Marilyn Ambra Thorpe on the stairway of the Bellevue Club in Oakland, California. (Photo: Laurie Gordon)

LOUISE BRADFORD AND PAUL SLOAN: A GATSBY SUMMER AFTERNOON

ouise Bradford and Paul Sloan took advantage of a perfect backdrop for their wedding—and they didn't mind sharing it with about one thousand uninvited guests. The couple married at the annual Gatsby Summer Afternoon at the Dunsmuir House & Gardens in Oakland, held in conjunction with the Art Deco Society of California.

Louise Bradford and Paul Sloan were wed at the Gatsby Summer Afternoon in September
1995. Here they take a victory lap around the Dunsmuir House & Gardens grounds,
expertly driven by Michael Heimovitz in his 1937 Lincoln.

(Photo: Nancy Eaton)

*A young Charleston dancer at the Gatsby
Summer Afternoon in Oakland, California.*

(Photo: Nancy Eaton)

Each year on a Sunday afternoon in early September, the gates of this fifty-acre estate open to admit hundreds of vintage automobiles (pre-1940 only, please) and revelers outfitted in 1910s to 1930s clothing. Some guests bring elaborate picnic setups, including wicker furniture, Oriental rugs, caged birds, portable Victrolas—even full sets of china, crystal, and silver. On an enormous parquet dance floor, partyers do the Lindy hop, Charleston, fox trot, and East Coast swing to Don Neely's eleven-member Royal Society Jazz Orchestra. And in the midst of this fabulous setting, it's not uncommon to spy a wedding party or two.

For weddings held at the Gatsby event, the ceremony is usually private, either at a separate place of worship or in a secluded part of the estate grounds, held just before the gates open to the public. A favorite spot for the I dos is at a charming little gazebo under the elms that fronts a pond in a small garden, just north of the main house. Afterward, the wedding party and guests can mingle with the rest of the partygoers, strolling the grounds to inspect all the fabulous vintage automobiles and picnic tableaux, or tour the beautifully restored thirty-seven-room Dunsmuir House, built in 1899.

Despite the ready-made setting and built-in entertainment, the Sloans found that having a wedding at the Gatsby picnic required a bit of effort. There are no on-site concessions, so they needed to bring their own food and beverages onto the grounds as well as tables and chairs for the wedding party and guests. They also needed to cover the picnic admission charge for each person.

If you like the setting but don't want the big crowd, the Dunsmuir House & Gardens hosts private weddings and receptions at other times of the year.

Louise Sloan recalls her wedding day at the Gatsby Summer Afternoon in 1995:

"I'd always loved the movie *It Happened One Night* with Claudette Colbert. There's that great scene at the beginning . . . you know the one, where she's wearing that beautiful early 1930s wedding dress . . . the scene where she goes overboard? That was one of the first movies I remember watching as a kid, and I think it had a big influence on me in developing a feel for the Art Deco period. I knew that was the era I wanted my wedding to be focused in.

"I found a great late 1930s wedding gown up in Benicia in this quaint little vintage clothing shop with its windows overlooking the harbor. I remember having a really good feeling about that day and such a good time. I got really lucky, because I found this dress, and it fit just perfectly. It didn't need any alterations. Paul wore a 1930s suit that we found in a shop in San Francisco. It had been worn by a groom in the early 1930s, and his wife had worn a gorgeous peach silk dress that was also for sale. The suit fit Paul and the dress fit me; it was remarkable, as if it were meant to be. So I bought the dress, too, and wore it on our anniversary.

"Paul and I had been to the Gatsby picnic the year before, and we really liked the atmosphere. We thought this would be a great way that our families and friends could have fun and have something to do at the reception, with the dancing and looking at everyone, with their picnics and great outfits. We brought in a little gazebo and set up our refreshments there for the wedding party. We kept with a vintage look by using those little Coke bottles and the IBC root beer in the old-fashioned bottles. And we had champagne, of course.

"Everything came together so beautifully. It's still great to think about how it all worked out so well. It was so nice to have the music and the picnic and everything else all done for us and not have to worry about much other than the food and drink for the guests and just having a good time."

C
H
A
P
T
E
R

EIGHT

wedding is a lot of hard work, and a vintage wedding presents its own special set of challenges. You may have thought about setting aside some of your budget to hire an events planner to help orchestrate your wedding so you can relax and enjoy yourself more. But how do you find the right person to work with? Is it important to hire a vintage events specialist? Can you get the same results working with an events generalist? What about a wedding coordinator?

First, think about what you really need. Is it someone to help you

The Aguilars seal their vintage vows with a kiss. (Photo: Laurie Gordon)

decide on a theme and research historical details? Someone to track down the right partners and vendors to execute the details? Someone to handle the logistics? You may need help with only some of this, but you may very well need help with it all.

WORKING WITH EVENTS SPECIALISTS

or help with the wedding theme and period details, it's beneficial to work with an events planner with historical event experience. Events planner Mary Litzinger is the founder of Vintage Productions, based in Los Angeles. She says that a vintage events consultant will help you make sure your event is historically accurate by recommending appropriate period details and will direct you to the most experienced vendors in your area who work in a period style. If you can't find a vintage events specialist where you live, she suggests interviewing a number of generalist events planners to find one with experience producing historical events as well as weddings. At your initial meeting, ask about the events they've done to see what kind of research was conducted, what recommendations were made from that research, and what the end results were. Get references and talk to former clients.

It's important to clear away any conceptual misunderstandings at the consultation meeting. Some planners hear the word *vintage,* and they immediately trot out all the obvious clichés—the flappers in fringe, the zoot suits, the gangsters, Marilyn Monroe and Elvis look-alikes, bobby sox, and poodle skirts. Find an events planner who appreciates the tasteful subtleties of vintage culture and doesn't just regurgitate a series of mainstream clichés. A good events consultant will show you lots of pictures and ask lots of questions in order to home in on what you really want. Be sure to bring any photos or ideas you have to the meeting, as well as this book.

Get leads for events planners from friends who have had successful weddings and from the public relations departments of corporations, museums, historical societies, Art Deco societies, and costume societies.

WORKING WITH A WEDDING COORDINATOR

f you have a good handle on your theme but need help implementing it, an events coordinator with wedding experience can help you. She should set you up with the most flexible and inventive bakers, florists, printers, and other vendors in your area, as these are the people more likely to know how to incorporate vintage concepts into their designs, rather than many mainstream vendors who tend to work in cookie-cutter style. The wedding coordinator will then manage all the details of your event once the design decisions have been made.

GOING IT ALONE

any people act as their own wedding planners and coordinators, and this can work out great if you have the time, the desire, and the expertise. You may already know enough about what you want that you don't need a lot of help. If you like doing research, are organized, and enjoy working with "subcontractors" and handling lots of details, there's no reason you can't do it on your own. There are some excellent wedding planning software programs on the market to help you stay on top of things.

SOME PARTING WORDS OF WISDOM

lanning and executing a big event is a daunting task, even for those who do it for a living. If you feel overwhelmed, realize that this is not easy for anybody, and allow yourself to make a mistake or two along the way without falling apart. This is supposed to be a happy time for you, so it helps to remember why you're doing this in the first place. Fashion designer Theresa LaQuey summed it up nicely:

"I think that the biggest problem is that all of a sudden brides start feeling like they're Flo Ziegfeld, managing the *Follies*. Most of them have never done anything on this scale before, and it's a lot to handle. They don't realize how stressful it is to put on a big show. They panic because they expect everything to be perfect, and nothing is ever perfect.

"It wasn't perfect for Ziegfeld, either. Chorus girls went out on stage in clothes held together by safety pins sometimes. This happens even to the best of professionals. You just have to let it go, accept that there will be times when things won't go perfectly and that this is okay.

"The most important thing is to remember why you're doing this in the first place. It's a wedding. It's about vows. You and your guy are tying the knot. That's what's most important. The rest of it is all icing, just frosting on the cake."

The LaQueys in a tender moment. (Photo: Laurie Gordon)

Have a wonderful vintage wedding. We'll be expecting a picture.

Resources

ere is a list of the resources featured in this book. You can find a more extensive and up-to-date list of worldwide vintage wedding resources on the official *Your Vintage Wedding* Web site, at www.retroactive.com/vintagewedding.html, where you can also share information with other prospective vintage brides.

INVITATIONS

Rock Scissor Paper
Susie and Heidi Bauer
Los Angeles, CA
(818) 361-1142
www.rockscissorpaper.com

Crane & Co., Inc.
30 South St.
Dalton, MA 01226
(800) 268-2281
www.crane.com

Crane's Online Wedding Blue Book
www.crane.com/social/weddings/
wedding-blue-book

VINTAGE-STYLE WEDDING PHOTOGRAPHY

The following photographers shot most of the contemporary photographs in this book.

Laurie Gordon
San Francisco, CA
(415) 566-2545

Ralph Granich
San Francisco, CA
(510) 839-3020

Scott Streble
San Francisco, CA
(800) 446-5358
(415) 339-9393 in California

Timothy Teague
Ojai, CA
(805) 646-0483

Cary Shapiro
Thousand Oaks, CA
(805) 371-8711

VINTAGE WEDDING GOWNS AND VEILS—ON-LINE RETAILERS

Antique & Vintage Dress Gallery
Deborah Burke
www.antiquedress.com

A Vintage Wedding
Donna Barr
www.vintagewedding.com

Gulden & Brown Antique Wedding Gowns
Lauren Lavonne Pritchett
www.gulden-brown.com
www.vintagegown.com

Cookie's Closet
www.cookiescloset.com

Everything Vintage
www.everythingvintage.com

Nancy's Nifty Nook
www.nancysniftynook.com

Victoria Rose Vintage Wedding Gowns
www.tias.com/stores/vr/
gowns-1.html

eBay
www.ebay.com

CUSTOM REPRODUCTION WEDDING GOWNS

Atelier Polonaise
Holly Hess and Shirley Kime craft historically accurate wedding gowns from the 1700s to the 1940s, using antique and reproduction silks and laces. They can work by mail, from

your measurements. Catalog price:
$13.00.
Toll-free within U.S.: (800) 618-7606
(619) 291-8709
www.victoriana.com/
Atelier_Polonaise

Theresa LaQuey
Theresa designs custom wedding
and evening gowns in the San
Francisco Bay area. She also creates
vintage-style dress patterns for
Simplicity.
(510) 635-6554
www.simplicity.com
Search for "adult costumes."

Dark Garden
321 Linden St.
San Francisco, CA 94102
(415) 431-7684
www.darkgarden.com

ZOOT SUITS
Siegel's Clothing Superstore
Sells and rents authentic
1930s–1940s zoot suits and
accessories. Creates made-to-order
zoot suits and pants.
2366 Mission St.
San Francisco, CA 94110
Toll-free within U.S.: (800) 408-8933
www.zootsuitstore.com

CORSETS
Dark Garden
321 Linden St.
San Francisco, CA 94102
(415) 431-7684
www.darkgarden.com

VINTAGE REPRODUCTION SHOES
Amazon Drygoods
Vintage shoes and boots. Catalog
price: $5.00.
2218 E. 11th St.
Davenport, IA 52803-3760
(319) 322-6800

VINTAGE SHOES
eBay
www.ebay.com

See also vintage clothing expos
and local vintage clothing stores in
your area.

SEMIANNUAL FASHION EXPOSITIONS
Vintage Fashion Expositions
Held in Santa Monica and San
Francisco every spring and fall.
(707) 793-0773

**San Francisco Art Deco Show
and Sale**
Held the first weekend of every June
and December.
(415) 383-3008

**Metropolitan Vintage and Antique
Textile Show**
Held four times a year in New York
City.
(212) 463-0200

VINTAGE AND REPRODUCTION
WEDDING DRESS PATTERNS

Amazon Drygoods
Patterns from the Past Catalog:
$5.00.
2218 E. 11th St.
Davenport, IA 52803-3760
(319) 322-6800

Folkwear Patterns
Edwardian through 1950s styles.
67 Broadway
Ashville, NC 28801
(800) 284-3388
www.larkbooks.com/home.nav/fw/
index.html

**eBay, Vintage Sewing Patterns
category**
www.ebay.com/aw/listings/list/all/
category4161/index.html

A Vintage Wedding
Donna Barr
(352) 377-0459
Toll-free within U.S.: (800) 660-3640
www.vintagewedding.com

Patterns from the Past
Michelle Lee
www.oldpatterns.com

Vintage Vogue
See your retailer for the complete
line; the Web site is usually not up-
to-date with the full selection. Find
these patterns at retail fabric stores.
www.voguepatterns.com/vintage
(800) 766-3619

VINTAGE FASHION RESEARCH

A Century in Shoes
www.centuryinshoes.com

**About.com's Historic
Reenactment Page**
reenactment.about.com/hobbies/
pastimes/reenactment/mbody.htm

Butterick/Vogue Pattern Archives
Archivists will research vintage styles and patterns from Butterick and Vogue on Monday and Thursday, 9:30 A.M. to 4:30 P.M. ET. The first twenty minutes of research are free, then $35/hour thereafter. (212) 620-2790

The Costume Gallery's Online Library
www.costumegallery.com/research.htm

VINTAGE GOWN RESTORATION AND PRESERVATION

Bruhn's Gown Restoration and Preservation
3939 La Vista Rd.
Tucker, GA 30084
(770) 939-2211
Toll-free within U.S.: (800) 833-4696
www.bruhnsbridal.com

DIE-STRUCK, HAND-ENGRAVED FILIGREE WEDDING RINGS

Antique Timepieces
574 San Anselmo Ave.
San Anselmo, CA 94960
(415) 454-4809
www.timepieces.com/jewelry.html

WEDDING CAKES

Cakework
Cecile Gady
San Francisco, CA
(415) 821-1333
www.cakework.com

Iced Delights
Gary Chapman
Surrey, United Kingdom
Tel: + 44 (0)208 541 0091
Fax: + 44 (0)208 851 3296
www.iceddelights.co.uk

Have Your Cake
Marilyn Tabatsky
Palo Alto, CA
(650) 873-8488

VINTAGE MUSIC ON CD

Past Perfect Records
Lower Farm Barns
Bainton Road
Bucknell
Oxon
OX6 9LT
UK
Tel: + 44 (0)186 932 5052
Fax: + 44 (0)186 932 5072
www.pastperfect.com

Rhino Records
www.rhino.com

MCA, Decca, and Hip-O Records
www.mca.com/lowmusic.html

Capitol's UltraLounge Series
www.ultralounge.com

Verve's Vintage Vault
www.verveinteractive.com

We also recommend these notable contemporary artists:

Vince Giordano's Nighthawks
1920s-style music.
www.riverwalk.org/profiles/
giordano.htm

Royal Society Jazz Orchestra
1920s-style music.
www.sonic.net/~rsjo

LaVay Smith and her Red Hot Skillet Lickers
1940s-style swing music.
www.lavaysmith.com

Big Bad Voodoo Daddy
1940s-style swing music.
www.bbvd.com

VINTAGE EVENT PRODUCTION
Laurie Gordon
(Northern California Only)
(415) 566-2545

Vintage Productions
Mary Litzinger
(Southern California Only)
(805) 492-2114

A GUIDE TO VINTAGE VENUES
The following vintage venues were mentioned in chapter 5. Prices we cited are subject to change. See the *Your Vintage Wedding* Web site for a more extensive list.

The Ebell of Los Angeles
743 S. Lucerne Blvd.
Los Angeles, CA 95005-3707
(323) 931-1277
www.ebellla.com

Palace of Fine Arts, San Francisco
Permits and Reservations
Department
3601 Lyon St.
San Francisco, CA 94123
(415) 831-5500

**Grand Central Station,
New York City**
New York Metropolitan Transit
Authority (MTA)
Vanderbilt Hall
Jones Lang LaSalle Management
Services, Inc.
150 Vanderbilt Ave., Hall 2A
New York, NY 10017
(212) 340-2347
www.grandcentralterminal.com

**The Empire State Building,
New York City**
Tricia Dempsey
350 Fifth Ave.
New York, NY 10118
(212) 736-3100, #377
www.esbnyc.com

Rosecliff, Newport, RI
The Preservation Society of Newport
County
424 Bellvue Ave.
Newport, RI 02840
(401) 847-2251
www.newportmansions.org

**The Astors' Beechwood Mansion
and Victorian Living History
Museum, Newport, RI**
580 Bellvue Ave.
Newport, RI 02840
(401) 846-3772
www.astors-beechwood.com

**The Palace Restaurant,
Sunnyvale, CA**
146 S. Murphy Ave.
Sunnyvale, CA 94086
(408) 739-5179
www.thepalacerestaurant.com

**The John and Mabel Ringling
Museum of Art, Sarasota, FL**
5401 Bay Shore Rd.
Sarasota, FL 34243
(941) 359-5700
www.ringling.org

Union Terminal, Cincinnati, OH
Jennifer Hillman, Director of Sales
1301 Western Ave.
Cincinnati, OH 45203
(513) 287-7004
www.cincymuseum.org

LOCATION SCOUTING (CALIFORNIA ONLY)

Here Comes the Guide

A comprehensive guide to wedding locations and wedding-related businesses in Northern or Southern California. A separate volume for each California geography. $19.95.

Hopscotch Press
PMB 135, 1563 Solano Ave.
Berkeley, CA 94707
(510) 525-3379
www.herecomestheguide.com

Bibliography

Belting, Natalia, and James R. Hine. *Your Wedding Work Book*. McKinley Foundation, 1958.

Gordon, Lois and Alan. *The Columbia Chronicles of American Life, 1910–1992*. New York: Columbia, 1995.

Home Arts and Entertainment. Chicago, Ill: Magazine Circulation Co., 1922.

The Ladies' Home Journal. June 1905.

Landsdell, Avril. *Wedding Fashions 1860–1980*. Buckinghamshire, UK: Shire, 1997.

LOOK magazine. May 23, 1939.

New York Gets Married, Exhibition Script. Museum of the City of New York, 1997.

New York Herald Tribune magazine. January 1, 1928.

Post, Emily. *Weddings*. New York: Pocket Books, 1963.

Tallman, Marjorie. *Dictionary of American Folklore*. New York: Philosophical Library, 1959.

Tober, Barbara. *The Bride: A Celebration*. Stamford, Conn.: Harry N. Abrams, 1984.

Vanderbilt, Amy. *Amy Vanderbilt's Complete Book of Etiquette*. Garden City, N.Y.: Doubleday, 1954.

Woods, Marjorie Binford. *Your Wedding: How to Plan and Enjoy It*. New York: Bobbs-Merrill, 1942.

Notes

NOTES

NOTES

NOTES